Twenty Thousand Years of New Mexico History

A Bibliography

Compiled and Annotated
with
An Ethnohistorical Introduction
by
Frances Leon Swadesh, PhD

SANTA FE

© 2016 by Frances Leon Swadesh
All Rights Reserved.
No part of this book may be reproduced in any form or by any electronic or mechanical means including information storage and retrieval systems without permission in writing from the publisher, except by a reviewer who may quote brief passages in a review.

Sunstone books may be purchased for educational, business, or sales promotional use. For information please write: Special Markets Department, Sunstone Press, P.O. Box 2321, Santa Fe, New Mexico 87504-2321.
Printed on acid-free paper
∞

Library of Congress Cataloging-in-Publication Data

Names: Quintana, Frances Leon.
Title: Twenty thousand years of New Mexico history : a bibliography / compiled and annotated with an ethnohistorical introduction by Frances Leon Swadesh, PhD.
Description: Santa Fe : Sunstone Press, 2015.
Identifiers: LCCN 2015043830 | ISBN 9780865346376 (softcover : alkaline paper)
Subjects: LCSH: New Mexico--History--Bibliography.
Classification: LCC Z1315 .Q85 2015 F796 | DDC 016.9789--dc23
LC record available at http://lccn.loc.gov/2015043830

SUNSTONE PRESS IS COMMITTED TO MINIMIZING OUR ENVIRONMENTAL IMPACT ON THE PLANET. THE PAPER USED IN THIS BOOK IS FROM RESPONSIBLY MANAGED FORESTS. OUR PRINTER HAS RECEIVED CHAIN OF CUSTODY (COC) CERTIFICATION FROM: THE FOREST STEWARDSHIP COUNCIL™ (FSC®), PROGRAMME FOR THE ENDORSEMENT OF FOREST CERTIFICATION™ (PEFC™), AND THE SUSTAINABLE FORESTRY INITIATIVE® (SFI®).
THE FSC® COUNCIL IS A NON-PROFIT ORGANIZATION, PROMOTING THE ENVIRONMENTALLY APPROPRIATE, SOCIALLY BENEFICIAL AND ECONOMICALLY VIABLE MANAGEMENT OF THE WORLD'S FORESTS. FSC® CERTIFICATION IS RECOGNIZED INTERNATIONALLY AS A RIGOROUS ENVIRONMENTAL AND SOCIAL STANDARD FOR RESPONSIBLE FOREST MANAGEMENT.

WWW.SUNSTONEPRESS.COM
SUNSTONE PRESS / POST OFFICE BOX 2321 / SANTA FE, NM 87504-2321 /USA
(505) 988-4418 / ORDERS ONLY (800) 243-5644 / FAX (505) 988-1025

TO DAISY SWADESH

with love and appreciation

TABLE OF CONTENTS

		Page
I.	GENERAL AND BACKGROUND INFORMATION	
	A. An Overview of New Mexico's Cultural Roots and Cross Cultural Contacts	1
	B. Bibliographies	20
	C. Archeology: General and Methodology	22
	D. History: General	23
	E. Pueblo Culture: Descriptive and General	24
	F. Navajo and Apache Culture: Descriptive and General	27
	G. Topography, Travel, Mineral Resources, Mining	29
II.	ARCHEOLOGY	
	A. Paleo-Indian Hunters and Archaic Desert Gatherers	32
	B. Anasazi	33
	C. Mogollon and Hohokam	40
	D. Navajo-Apache	43
	E. Ute	44
	F. Hispano	44
III.	SPANISH COLONIAL AND MEXICAN PERIOD (1540-1846)	
	A. Exploration by Spaniards, First Encounters with Indians (1540-1592)	44
	B. Indian Experience of Colonialism	46
	1. Pueblos	46
	2. Navajo-Apache	47
	3. Utes and Plains Tribes	49
	C. Hispanic New Mexico	50
	D. Anglo Penetration and Conquest	55
IV.	TERRITORIAL PERIOD (1846-1912)	
	A. Pueblos: Trespass	58
	B. Navajo-Apaches: Wars	58
	C. Hispanos: Land Loss	60
	D. Anglos	62
	1. Civil War	62
	2. Frontier Violence	62
	3. Ranching, Business and Transportation	63
	4. Administration and Statehood Question	65

V.	RECENT HISTORY: CHANGE IN CULTURE AND INSTITUTIONS	
	A. General	66
	B. Pueblos	68
	C. Navajo-Apache	71
	D. Hispano	73
VI.	INTERGROUP RELATIONS	77
VII.	ARTS AND SKILLS	
	A. General	80
	B. Textiles and Basketry	
	General	82
	Pueblo	82
	Navajo-Apache	83
	Hispano	84
	Anglo	85
	C. Pottery	
	Pueblo	86
	Navajo-Apache	87
	Hispano	88
	Anglo	88
	D. Pictorial and Decorative Arts	
	General	88
	Pueblo	90
	Navajo-Apache	91
	Hispano	91
	Anglo	93
	E. Architecture and House Interiors	
	General	94
	Pueblo	95
	Navajo-Apache	95
	Hispano	95
	Anglo	97
	F. Music-Dance-Drama-Ritual and Poetry	
	General	98
	Pueblo	99
	Navajo-Apache	100
	Hispano	102
	G. Storytelling-Myths-Healing	
	General	104
	Pueblo	104
	Navajo-Apache	105
	Hispano	108

	H. Plants-Animals-Food	
	General	109
	Pueblo	110
	Navajo-Apache	111
	Hispano	112
	I. Warfare and Hunting	
	General	112
	Pueblo	113
	Navajo-Apache	113
	Hispano	113
	Anglo	113
	J. Recreation: Games, Riddles, Jokes	
	Pueblo	113
	Navajo-Apache	114
	Hispano	114
VIII.	LIST OF APPOINTED AND ELECTED GOVERNORS OF NEW MEXICO (1598-1974)	115
IX.	LIST OF MUSEUMS AND MONUMENTS IN NEW MEXICO	118
	AUTHOR INDEX	122

ACKNOWLEDGMENTS

The following bibliography does not pretend to be exhaustive. It was compiled by the author with the substantial help of colleagues on the staff of the Museum of New Mexico and many other friends. Our purpose was to bring together for the interested general reader, for teachers and for students in high schools and junior colleges a listing that would reflect the multicultural richness that is New Mexico.

The bibliography was originally proposed by Ruth Elvin whose devoted custody of the desk at the Palace of the Governors has brought her into daily contact with people seeking knowledge of New Mexico. Her experience provided the subject classification which organizes the Table of Contents. Among the many contributors of titles and annotations in their fields of expertise, the following names must be mentioned with particular gratitude: Mary Bryan, Benito Cordova, Evelyn Ely, Nancy Fox, Alden Hayes, Phyllis Hughes, David Kayser, Stewart Peckham, Edna Robertson, Marc Simmons, Ron Stewart, Betty Toulouse, Helene Warren, Michael Weber and John Wilson. For errors in judgment, citation and orthography, the author accepts full responsibility.

ABBREVIATION CODE: PUBLICATION TITLES FREQUENTLY CITED

AA: American Anthropologist

AAAM: Memoirs of the American Anthropological Association

AMNH: American Museum of Natural History

BAE: Bureau of American Ethnology

MNM: Museum of New Mexico, Santa Fe

NMHR: New Mexico Historical Review

NMQR: New Mexico Quarterly Review

NPS: National Park Service

PPMAAE: Papers of the Peabody Museum of Archeology and Ethnology

SAR: School of American Research

SWJA: Southwestern Journal of Anthropology

UNM: University of New Mexico

I. GENERAL AND BACKGROUND

A. AN OVERVIEW OF NEW MEXICO'S CULTURAL ROOTS AND CROSS CULTURAL CONTACTS

In all the United States New Mexico is unmatched for the depth of its traditions and for its multicultural network. The state is a veritable laboratory for study of the ways groups of men have met and influenced one another. The bibliography which follows provides a fairly inclusive but far from complete listing of the best published sources testifying to New Mexico's record of cultural continuity and intercultural mingling. Many good readings not listed are either unpublished, difficult to obtain or more technical than the readings offered.

The New Mexico record also provides examples of a variety of adaptations to a difficult and challenging environment. These adaptations are reflected in settlement patterns, uses of natural resources, specialized technologies, social organization and philosophical systems.

Except for Section VI, Intergroup Relations, each section of the bibliographical listing is subdivided by ethnic group. Because of the high temporal priority of Indian settlement in New Mexico, there are listings throughout for the Pueblos and Navajo-Apaches, whereas the listings for Anglo-Americans are sparser.

Anglo-Americans came to New Mexico only one and a half centuries ago, bringing with them a set of culture traits which had evolved in a vastly different environment. In the brief time that Anglos have been here, little adaptation to New Mexico has occurred, although Section VII-D, Pictorial Arts, deals with a regional school of Anglo artists. Section VII-B, Textiles and Basketry, and Section VII-C, Pottery, on the other hand, have Anglo entries which refer to styles and techniques of nationwide rather than specifically New Mexican occurrence.

New Mexico's culture history began some 20,000 years ago with the presence of big-game hunters of the Late Pleistocene period, a time of more abundant plant and animal life and water resources than at the present. This culture is called <u>Paleo-Indian</u>, although the lack of human remains in the kill sites and hearth sites which define the culture makes it impossible to describe their physical type. Such sites are largely found east of the Rocky Mountains from northern Colorado to Central Mexico.

Some 9,000 years ago, a more arid climate began to prevail and big game became scarce. A culture known as <u>Archaic Desert</u>, already widespread west of the Rocky Mountains, spread eastward into New Mexico. Archaic Desert people hunted small game but subsisted in large numbers by gathering wild plant foods which they milled on large stones with a slight hollow, called <u>metates</u>, using smaller grinding stones, called <u>manos</u>.

Due to the lack of skeletal remains for this period, it

is impossible to say whether the Archaic Desert people of New Mexico were a population new to the area or whether the local Paleo-Indians simply adopted the subsistence patterns of neighboring peoples when the big game vanished. Recent excavations in the area of Tomé and the Río Puerco, however, have unearthed remains of mammoth and extinct bison bones in association with stone implements for scraping, chopping and milling such as are diagnostic of the Archaic Desert culture. This suggests that big-game hunters and food gatherers, if not actually the same people, at least lived together in some instances (see Section II-A of the Bibliography).

Knowledge of the cultivation of corn had reached southwestern New Mexico more than 4,000 years ago, in consequence to its cultivation in Central Mexico. The cultivation of beans and squash began in New Mexico 1,000 years later. Southwestern New Mexico and southeastern Arizona were also the setting for a prehistoric Pueblo (village) farming culture, the Mogollon, which has left us remains of pit-houses and pottery dating from as early as 200 B.C.

In the early centuries of the Christian Era, in the Four Corners area where New Mexico, Colorado, Utah and Arizona meet, there were pit-house settlements of farmers whose culture exemplifies what is known of the Basketmaker phase of the Anasazi culture, a forerunner of the New Mexico Pueblos. The Anasazi people first produced pottery under the influence of the Mogollon people and were not directly under the influence of developments further south in Mexico. Like the

Mogollons, the Anasazis appear to have developed their way of life directly out of the Archaic Desert culture since food gathering and the hunting of small game continued to be important to their subsistence pattern, and the ubiquitous <u>metate</u> and <u>mano</u> continued to be the most important implements for the processing of foods.

In southwestern Arizona, during the first millenium of the Christian era, a village culture emerged with distinctively Mexican traits borrowed from more urbanized societies to the south. This was the <u>Hohokam</u> culture, known for its rudimentary temple mounds, ceremonial ball courts, practice of irrigation agriculture, cremation of the dead and other features, some of which eventually spread to the Anasazis.

By the eleventh century A.D. all three cultures were at the height of their development as Classic prehistoric Pueblo communities. A large and rapid increase in population occurred. Great stone multi-family apartment dwellings were built in the Anasazi and Mogollon areas. Ceremonial chambers called <u>kivas</u> were also built, usually underground like the pit-house dwellings and, in the case of the Anasazis, usually circular. By the thirteenth century, the large Pueblos were abandoned and population movement began to bring a large population of Pueblos into the Rio Grande Valley, hitherto sparsely populated.

It is believed that the Anasazis were the ancestors of today's Tanoan Pueblos who still live in the Rio Grande drainage and whose languages are distantly related to the great Uto-

Aztecan family. These Pueblos have three linguistic subdivisions. The Tiwas include Taos, Picurís, Sandía and Isleta Pueblos; the Tewas are San Juan, Santa Clara, San Ildefonso, Nambé, Pojoaque and Tesuque Pueblos; the Towas are Jemez and, formerly, Pecos Pueblos. It is also believed that the Hohokams were the ancestors of today's Pimas and, possibly, their close linguistic relatives, the Papagos.

The origins of modern-day Keresan and Zuñi Indians are obscure and still under active debate, although archeologists currently believe that Keresan forebears built the great apartment complexes of Mesa Verde, Aztec and Chaco Canyon. Keresan speech is considered an affiliate of the Hokan-Coahuiltecan family of languages, very ancient and widespread in North America. Zuñi has been variously linked with Aztec-Tanoan, Penutian and even Macro-Quechuan, whose main center is Andean. The Hopis of Arizona speak a Shoshonean language of the Uto-Aztecan family, hence are closer linguistic relatives of the nomadic Utes and Comanches than they are of the Tanoan Pueblos. At the same time, the nomadic Kiowas speak a language identified as Tanoan.

When the first Spanish explorers met the Pueblos in the middle of the sixteenth century, the Tanoans were still moving into the Rio Grande Valley from the northwest, and the Keresans were moving in from the west. All the present-day Pueblos (with the possible exception of Laguna, which may have been at that time a small hamlet dependent upon Acoma) were settled and there were many more villages than exist today. The Pueblo

Indians lived in compact villages and practised a well-developed subsistence agriculture founded on the cultivation of maize, beans and squash. They also hunted and gathered many wild plant foods. All the Tanoan Pueblos and the Keresans within the Rio Grande drainage (Cochití, Santo Domingo, San Felipe, Santa Ana and Sía) built irrigation ditches to water their crops. It is believed that they adopted irrigation from the Hohokams during the period of migration to the Río Grande Valley, a time of extensive drouth and curtailment of the growing season. At the time the Spaniards came, the total Pueblo population has been variously estimated as between 40,000 and 60,000 (see Sections II-A and III-A).

By the middle of the fifteenth century, the Pueblos were no longer the sole occupants of New Mexico. The southern branch of Athapaskan speakers, later to become differentiated into Navajos and the various branches of Apaches -- the Western Apaches, Chiricahuas, Mescaleros, Jicarillas, Lipans and Kiowa Apaches of today -- began to filter into New Mexico from the north, both east and west of the Rocky Mountains. In both language and culture, they differed markedly from the Pueblos. They were roving hunters and food gatherers and, shortly after first contact with the Pueblos, they began to raid the Pueblos at harvest time (see Sections II-D and III-A).

With the exception of the Mescaleros, most Apachean (Southern Athapaskan) bands learned from their Pueblo neighbors, as time went on, how to raise corn. Only the Navajos, however, from intimate contact with Pueblos in the late seventeenth and early eighteenth centuries, became serious farmers who raised vegetables and a variety of fruits introduced to the Pueblos by the Spaniards. The Navajos, and other Apacheans to a lesser extent, adopted certain features of the Pueblo religion which they rewove into their dominant cultural themes of warding off disease and restoring health, rather than adopting the Pueblo theme of fertility in an arid environment.

Despite Apache raiding, friendly relations developed between certain Pueblos and certain Apache bands, especially east of the Río Grande. The Apache bands that hunted buffalo on the eastern plains of New Mexico provided the Pueblos with meat and hides, for which the Pueblos traded their produce and woven cotton cloth (see Sections II-D and VI).

The large military expedition of Francisco Vasquez de Coronado penetrated to the heart of the Pueblo country in the fall of 1540 after a hostile reception by the Zuñis of western New Mexico. The year previous, the Zuñis had killed Estebanico of Fray Marcos de Niza's advance scouting party. The high-handed demands of Coronado's officers for food, clothes and women placed upon the Tiwa pueblo of Tiguex, north of Albuquerque, a burden which the Indians were unwilling to carry. They attacked the Spaniards who retaliated savagely, putting several hundred Tiwas to death.

As a result of this slaughter, a number of Tiwa pueblos were abandoned, the Indians taking to the mesa-tops to resist their would-be conquerors. Any warlike gesture of later Spanish explorers was resisted by force. Once they had overcome their fear of the Spaniards' horses and cannon, the Pueblos defended their independence more effectively than the Indians of Central Mexico, because they were not subject to the rule of a monarch. Each village was a completely autonomous unit whose leadership was theocratic, deeply committed to a particular way of life. The social integration and durability of the Pueblos made it possible for them to resist being swamped by societies of greater economic and military development, with minimum adjustments, using their capacity to live in the Archaic Desert style for purposes of evading subjugation. In the sixteenth century, the Pueblos commenced a process of re-grouping for purposes of defense against both Apaches and Spaniards (see Sections I-D, III-A and III-B).

Juan de Oñate's pioneer Spanish settlement, founded at the Tewa village of Oke (San Juan Pueblo), then at Yuqueyunque (later San Gabriel) in 1598, imposed conditions which could only stimulate Pueblo resistance, sowing the seeds from which eventually exploded the 1680 Pueblo Revolt. Military leaders under Oñate received <u>encomiendas</u>, authority over certain stretches of land near a given Pueblo from whose population they could requisition labor on the assigned land. Products of this labor went largely to the <u>encomendero</u>. The governors of New Mexico exacted tribute in kind and in labor for the Crown, much of which certain governors appropriated for their own profit. The Franciscan missionaries, too, required labor of the Pueblo Indians for construction of mission churches, cultivation of mission lands and care of livestock which, in part, furnished subsistence for the mission fathers.

Added to the burden of forced labor, attempts were made to extirpate the Pueblo religion by force, as well as by preachment. Kivas were sacked, the masks and representations of supernatural beings called kachinas were burned and religious leaders were chastised and even put to death. These indignities provoked the Revolt (see Sections III-B and III-C).

From 1680 to 1692 there was no Spanish settlement in New Mexico, as the refugees from the Pueblo Revolt regrouped in Guadalupe del Paso, and successive military expeditions were sent to try to beat the Pueblos into submission. Some Pueblos did bow to terrorism while others continued to resist. When Diego de Vargas began his finally successful re-entry in 1692, he combined military measures with much bargaining and persuasion which finally secured from the Pueblos permission for the Spanish settlement to return. The Pueblos did insist, however, on compliance with the Laws of the Indies which banned the encomienda system and forced, uncompensated labor by Indians. The Pueblos also demanded that certain settlers whose past actions had outraged them be forbidden to return.

After the return of the Spanish colony, there were lesser revolts and some Pueblos continued to be deserted until the early eighteenth century, the Indians living on high mesas or, as in the case of Jemez Indians, living with the Navajos. During this period of uncertainty and fear, numerous Pueblo Indians seem to have assimilated into one or another nomadic tribe since the Pueblo population declined sharply while the nomadic population rose.

De Vargas brought about 100 soldiers and 800 settlers into New Mexico in the fall of 1693, many of them selected from volunteers who resided in the City and Valley of Mexico. Only some 40 families of pre-Revolt settlers returned. The new settlers were called <u>Españoles Mexicanos</u> because, while Spanish in culture, they had been born and raised in Mexico and many were descendants of conquistadors and their Indian wives. These settlers raised maize and ground it with a metate and mano, like the Indians of Mexico and the Pueblos of New Mexico.

The families of <u>Españoles Mexicanos</u> and others who were brought to New Mexico in June, 1694, by Fray Francisco Farfán, as well as 27 more families brought in 1695 from Zacatecas, Fresnillo and Sombrerete in the mineral-rich mountains of northern Mexico, were farmers and ranchers who had been selected for their skills and for the example of sobriety and Christian piety it was hoped they would provide for their Indian neighbors.

The settlers who came with de Vargas were given land grants to form new communities. Some single families received grants but, more commonly, a grant was made to a group of families, and their title was only confirmed after they had built homes, dug irrigation ditches, planted crops, served in the local militia and resided on the grant for several years. Each grantee family received an allotment of land on which to build a home and raise crops, but each community had areas of common land, both within the village and in the surrounding hills and forests, which represented the principal acreage of community grants. Here livestock was grazed on the unfenced range, and the settlers gathered wild plants and firewood, as well as cutting timbers for their houses, furniture and implements.

Regulations required that the settlers form tight-knit communities around a central plaza, with intersecting streets forming a grid-plan. Most land-grant communities developed, however, as a series of small, kin-based <u>placitas</u> built above the easily cultivable islands of irrigable land in the usually narrow river valleys. The number of nuclear families in a <u>placita</u> ranged from less than a dozen to more than 50, with all residents sharing a great part of their subsistence activities. After men had cleared the fields, women, children and the elderly tended crops. Teenage youths and men engaged in care of livestock on the mountain range, in buffalo hunting and trading with the Indians, in militia service and in accompanying the annual trade caravans to Chihuahua and other Mexican cities.

The small, isolated villages of New Mexico were very much on their own for subsistence and survival in the eighteenth century. Goods imported from Mexico, even such items as nails and paper, were in the luxury class. Villagers grew all their own food, wove their homespun wool for clothing and often used buckskin garments patterned after Plains Indian garb. Those who owned shoes, by and large, saved them for special occasions and walked barefoot or wore teguas (Indian moccasins) on ordinary days.

Village craftsmen, such as hatmakers, saintmakers and blacksmiths, worked their farms like their neighbors and devoted only part of their time to their craft. Class distinctions were less prominent in New Mexico than in most areas of Latin-America because life was laden with both opportunity and hazard on the northern frontier of New Spain. A wealthy man might lose all his property in one Indian raid, while a poor man, by taking booty in raids against the nomadic Indians or by trading with them, might become affluent. There was no hereditary nobility in New Mexico except for the appointed civil leaders who remained only a few years. According to accounts from both the Colonial and Mexican periods, the people of New Mexico had little wealth but no class of beggars.

The way of life that developed in eighteenth century New Mexico was one of profound and diverse intercultural contact which took place in a context rather different from the usual situation in colonial lands. The Spanish-speaking settlers were in a decided minority until late in the century and were in no position to impose their way of life on the Indians, least of all the nomadic groups. Transmission of Hispanic culture elements occurred in a variety of ways.

The Tanoan and Keresan Pueblos and, to a lesser extent,

the Zuñis accepted Catholicism as transmitted by the Franciscan fathers but maintained their traditional religion intact, as a separate entity. The sacred masked dance-dramas were performed in the privacy of the kivas, from which outsiders were excluded (except for the Shalako dance of the Zuñis). The Hopis refused to permit the return of the Franciscans and, to this day, perform their masked dances in public. The Spaniards imposed forms of religious and civil leadership on the Pueblos, with the exception of the Hopi villages, but the officers who represented Spanish authority in the Pueblos were selected by the Pueblo theocratic leaders. The internal structure of Pueblo society, therefore, was little affected.

From the Spaniards, the Pueblos learned to cultivate new crops, including tree fruits of European origin and chile and tomatoes from Mexico. They never abandoned their basic "CBS" (corn-beans-squash) subsistence pattern. They modified their clothing somewhat to suit Spanish tastes but kept their traditional garments. The costumes used for ritual dances especially were little modified (see Sections I-D and V-B).

The subject peoples of colonial societies have tended to become a subordinate class and, in some instances, chattel slaves. This fate fell to a small percentage of Pueblo Indians during the seventeenth and early eighteenth centuries when Pueblo war captives were kept as servants by the more affluent settlers.

Servitude in settler homes may have brought about the hispanization of some Pueblo Indians, but the record indicates that many more adopted Spanish ways while living in their home villages. The Pueblo leadership rejected and expelled those who became overly hispanicized, forcing them to move to the Spanish settlements or to communities established under Colonial regulations for the Pueblos to accommodate detribalized Indians. These detribalized Indians, called <u>Genízaros</u>, had usually been ransomed from captivity among the nomadic tribes and received grants of land at the far periphery of settlement on condition that they serve in the militia. Those <u>Genízaros</u> who won sufficient booty in raids against the nomadic Indians became able to buy private lands and acquire <u>vecino</u> (tithes-paying settler) status. Detribalized Pueblo Indians also followed this path, eventually becoming identified as "Spaniards". This, plus the ravages of contagious diseases of European origin, accounts for the drop in Pueblo population from 12,142 in 1750 to 9,732 in 1799, while the population labelled "Spanish and Castas" vastly increased.

For Indians other than the Pueblos, the pattern of change was of a different order. On the buffalo plains, life was completely revolutionized by the use of the horse. Individual horsemen singled out their prey, overtook it from the rear and speared it between the ribs with a backward thrust, the "Parthian Shot", introduced to Spain no doubt by the Visigoths. The techniques of hunting from horseback were no doubt taught the Indians by settlers who, in turn, learned the habits of buffalo from the Indians. Only the Comanches learned the art of horse-breeding from the Spaniards. All Plains Indians remained free of Spanish political or social domination.

The Navajos also acquired the horse, but its importance in their society was largely focussed on the prestige gained by young men through horse-racing and gambling on the outcome. Sheep, on the other hand, profoundly transformed Navajo culture. Seasonal shifts in residence were now geared to grazing needs. The Navajos became skilled weavers of woolen cloth. It is a question whether Navajo skills in sheepraising and weaving were the outcome more of Navajo captivity in Spanish settlements or of the flight of renegade settlers to Navajo camps. In weaving, at least, the Navajos invented their own loom form and distinctive techniques and patterns. The Navajos as a group did not adopt Christianity nor become subjected to Spanish authority, except to the extent that some groups agreed to treaties.

The Spanish settlers were influenced by contact with Indians in many ways beyond the obvious fact that part-Indian ancestry was common among them, both from Mexican and New Mexican sources. The eighteenth century settlers were well versed in irrigation agriculture and other means of survival in an arid land, in living among Indians and in adjusting to new circumstances, all skills learned by their ancestors in Mexico. They borrowed from the Pueblos the use of many wild plants for food and medicines and also adopted from the Indians the cutting and drying of deer and buffalo meat in thin strips to make jerky. They virtually abandoned their use of clumsy firearms and tactics of pitched battle in favor of the bows and arrows and surprise raid tactics of the Indians. Like the Plains tribes, they took prisoners whom they often adopted into the family. The forms of house construction they used combined Old and New World principles.

Perhaps the deepest way in which contact with Indians affected the Spanish-speaking settlers of New Mexico was the attitude toward land which they acquired, an attitude also found in the Mestizo villages of Mexico most integrated with neighboring Indians. People feel that they have a mystic link with the land that they till: "The land is our mother". Such a sacramental feeling is still found in New Mexico, especially in relation to the community lands of the Hispanic villages, lands which were to be shared by all and never alienated from the community.

The colonial settlements of New Mexico, unlike those of Mexico and other areas of the New World, did not grow into large towns but tended to multiply into new, scattered communities, hamlets rather than villages. This settlement pattern was undoubtedly conditioned by the same environmental factors which shaped the distribution of the Pueblo riverine communities. Only narrow islands of bottomland could be cleared and irrigated with the simple implements at hand. Along the Río Grande and its tributary streams, such easily cultivated lands were scattered, and each could only support a limited population. For the settlers, there was the additional consideration of the range areas needed to raise livestock. A further inducement to the movement of population outward beyond the periphery of settlement was the attraction of trade with nomadic Indians.

The triumph of Mexico's struggle for independence in 1821 set in motion changes in New Mexico which had been foreshadowed by the short-lived liberal Spanish Constitution of 1812. Representative government with full manhood suffrage was instituted, including both detribalized and Pueblo Indians. At the same time, the nascent Mexican Republic, weakened by the internal pressures of factionalism, began to experience ever-growing pressure from her powerful northern neighbor, the United States.

These pressures were most directly experienced in the Mexican Territories of Texas and New Mexico which were soon deeply penetrated by United States business interests. Texas fell first, in 1836, then New Mexico and California, in 1846, barely a quarter century after Mexican independence (see Sections III-B, III-C, and III-D).

The arrival in New Mexico of military forces in 1846 and, in later years, of civil administrators and businessmen brought into being a government and dominant society of a very different order from the majority of Spanish-speaking and Indian institutions of New Mexico. While the Anglo-American segment of the population was for many years sparse in New Mexico, its influence far exceeded its numbers. In 1850 there were less than 1,000 Anglos compared with some 50,000 Hispanos, 9,000 Pueblos and many thousands of Navajos, Apaches, Utes and other Indians in New Mexico. The Indian population total may well have equalled that of the Hispanos.

The United States military occupation of New Mexico, coupled with the overbearing pressures of westward movement of population from the eastern seaboard, stimulated chronic warfare between western nomadic Indians and non-nomadic populations. In New Mexico, a war of extermination was conducted, first against the Navajos and, for 30 years, against the Apaches, with artificial stimulation exerted by the Civil War. By the end of this period, the Navajos and Apaches had been forced onto reservations in New Mexico and Arizona; the Utes, Comanches and Kiowas had been altogether expelled from New Mexico, and the Pueblos and Spanish-speaking New Mexicans had been deprived of a great deal of their land. Some lands were seized by force, but even more were lost in a process of legalistic maneuvering.

During this period, Anglo-American ranchers moved in from Texas and other states and, while continuing small in numbers, imposed their way of life with considerable show of violence. From 1850 to 1912, despite her permanent settled population and her villages and towns with orderly systems of internal control, New Mexico remained a territory, controlled through Congress by a handful of powerful men (see Section IV).

As late as 1940, Anglo-Americans still did not equal the combined numbers of Hispanos and Indians in the population of New Mexico but, by that time, many irrevocable changes had occurred due to the influence of Anglo culture (see Sections V and VI). What is remarkable is that, despite the winds of change, New Mexico's traditional cultures have managed to survive and today continue to maintain their vitality and influence. Section VII of the Bibliography is an inventory of sources on the arts and skills of the past, many of which continue in active practice.

Anglo-Americans of the Southwest have benefited greatly from such Hispanic subsistence skills as the ranching and mining methods which continue to be practiced in New Mexico, as in generations past, (see Section IV-D) but these skills have now been incorporated into a society in which production is geared to profit. Many Indians and Hispanos have preserved their cultural orientation toward subsistence and living in harmony with nature rather than exploitation of resources for maximum profit. As the Anglo-American society becomes more aware of the need for ecological management, we may come to appreciate the adaptations made in the past to New Mexico's fragile and demanding environment.

B. BIBLIOGRAPHIES

1. BOLTON, HERBERT E.: Guide to Materials for the History of the United States in the Principal Archives of Mexico. Washington, D.C.: Carnegie Institution, Publication No. 163, 1913.

2. CAMPA, ARTHUR L.: A Bibliography of Spanish Folk-Lore in New Mexico. Albuquerque, UNM Language Series, Bulletin No. 2/3, 1930.

3. CHAPMAN, CHARLES E.: Catalogue of Materials in the Archivo General de Indias for the History of the Pacific Coast and the American Southwest. Berkeley: University of California Publications in History, Vol. 8, 1919.

4. CHAVEZ, FRAY ANGELICO: Archives of the Archdiocese of Santa Fe, 1678-1900. Washington, D.C.: Academy of American Franciscan History, 1957.

> Index of materials available on microfilm at the State Records Center, Santa Fe, New Mexico.

5. COMPREHENSIVE INDEX TO NMHR.: Lansing B. Bloom: Vol. I: covers Vols. 1-15 (1926-1940), 1941.

> Frank D. Reeve: Vol. II: covers Vols. 16-30 (1941-1956), 1956.

> In Press: Vol. III (to cover 1957-1970).
> Albuquerque: Historical Society of New Mexico and UNM Press. These volumes are handy locators for articles in the New Mexico Historical Review not listed in this bibliography.

6. CORRELL, J. LEE, EDITHA L. WATSON and DAVID M. BRUGGE: Navajo Bibliography with Subject Index. Revised Edition in two volumes. Window Rock, Arizona: The Navajo Tribe, 1969.

7. DIAZ, ALBERT JAMES: "Bibliography of Bibliographies Relating to the History and Literature of New Mexico". New Mexico Magazine 36/1: 56ff., 1958.

8. MAJOR, MABEL and T. M. PEARCE: Southwest Heritage, A Literary History with Bibliography. Albuquerque: UNM Press, 1970.

9. NEW MEXICO STATE LIBRARY: <u>Spanish Heritage in New Mexico</u>. Santa Fe: New Mexico State Library, 1972.
Materials listed cover art, architecture, armor, cowboys and horses, drama, folklore, genealogy, historical fiction, history and many other topics, including children's literature and films in the collections of the State Library. A joint work by members of the Library Staff.

10. POWELL, LAURENCE C.: <u>Southwestern Book Trails: A Reader's Guide to the Heartland of New Mexico and Arizona</u>. Albuquerque: Horn and Wallace, 1963. A readable introduction to southwestern bibliography.

11. RITTENHOUSE, JACK D.: <u>New Mexico Civil War Bibliography</u>. Houston: Stagecoach Press, 1971.
Annotated list of 32 basic works.

12. RITTENHOUSE, JACK D.: <u>The Santa Fe Trail: A Historical Bibliography</u>. Albuquerque: UNM Press, 1971.
718 annotated titles and an index of congressional documents on the subject.

13. SACCONAGHI, CHARLES D.: "A Bibliographical Note on the Civil War in the West". <u>Arizona and the West 8: 349-364, 1966</u>.
Supplements Rittenhouse's Civil War bibliography.

14. SAUNDERS, LYLE A.: <u>A Guide to Materials Bearing on the Cultural Relations in New Mexico</u>. Albuquerque: UNM Press, 1944.
While outdated, this is an excellent source.

15. SCHOLES, FRANCE V.: "Manuscripts for the History of New Mexico in the National Library of Mexico City." <u>NMHR 3/3: 301-323, 1928</u>.
For the serious historical scholar.

16. THESES AND DISSERTATIONS, UNM: <u>See Subject Card File in the Social Sciences Division</u>. Albuquerque: Zimmerman Library, UNM.

17. THOMASSON, CAROL J. ET AL: <u>New Mexico History Bibliography for the General Reader</u>. Albuquerque: Zimmerman Library, UNM, 1966. Special Collections Department.

18. TULLY, MARJORIE F. and JUAN B. RAEL: <u>An Annotated Bibliography of Spanish Folklore in New Mexico and Colorado</u>. Albuquerque: Zimmerman Library, UNM, 1950. Special Collections.

19. TWITCHELL, RALPH E.: The Spanish Archives of New Mexico, 2 Vols. Cedar Rapids, Iowa: The Torch Press, 1914.
Vol. I lists documents referring to land; these documents are available on microfilm at BLM, UNM and other places, as indexed in Albert J. Diaz, A Guide to the Microfilm of Papers Relating to the New Mexico Land Grants, Albuquerque: University of New Mexico Press, 1960. Vol. II lists documents referring to administration, microfilmed at the State Records Center, Santa Fe. Twitchell's descriptions of the documents he indexed are in some instances inaccurate.

20. WAGNER, HENRY R.: The Spanish Southwest, 1542-1794, 2 Vols. Albuquerque: UNM Press, 1937.
The most comprehensive listing extant of Spanish Colonial sources.

21. ZIMMERMAN LIBRARY, UNM: Manuscripts and Records in the University of New Mexico Library. Albuquerque: UNM, 1957.

C. ARCHEOLOGY: GENERAL AND METHODOLOGY
(See also Sections II and VII-B through E, passim)

22. CERAM, C.W.: The First American: A Story of North American Archeology. New York: Harcourt Brace-Jovanovich, Inc., 1971.
Informal and anecdotal, with profuse illustrations and extensive coverage of the Southwest.

23. JENNINGS, JESSE D. and EDWARD NORBECK, eds.: Prehistoric Man in the New World. Chicago: University of Chicago Press, 1964.
An outstanding collection of symposium papers, with particularly good coverage of the Southwest.

24. LISTER, FLORENCE C. and ROBERT H.: Earl Morris and Southwestern Archeology. Albuquerque: UNM Press, 1969.
Readable book on archeology and archeologists, with explanation of the development of methodology to reconstruct time sequences.

25. MANGELSDORF, PAUL C., RICHARD S. MACNEISH and WELTON C. GALENAL: "Domestication of Corn". Science 143/3606: 538-545, 1964.
Important information on analysis of corn cultivated 4,000 years ago, discovered in Bat Cave, southwestern New Mexico.

26. SCHOENWETTER, JAMES: How Old Is It? Dating in Archeology. Santa Fe: UNM Press, 1965. Popular Pamphlet, No. 2.

27. SMILEY, T. L., STANLEY A. STUBBS and B. BANNISTER: <u>A Foundation for the Dating of Some Late Archeological Sites in the Rio Grande Area, New Mexico</u>. Tucson, Arizona: Laboratory of Tree Ring Research, Bulletin No. 6, 1953.

28. WILLEY, GORDON R.: <u>An Introduction to American Archeology</u>. Englewood Cliffs, New Jersey: Prentiss-Hall, 1966.

D. GENERAL HISTORY

29. BANCROFT, HUBERT: <u>History of Arizona and New Mexico 1530-1888</u>. San Francisco: The History Company, 1889. (Reprinted, 1962 by Horn and Wallace, Albuquerque).
A classic, based on many primary materials, of which some have since disappeared. Still considered a good source.

30. BANDELIER, ADOLPH A.: <u>Southwestern Journals of Adolph A. Bandelier, Vol. I, 1880-1882</u>. Charles H. Lange and Carroll L. Riley, eds. Albuquerque: UNM Press and SAR, 1966.

31. BANDELIER, ADOLPH A.: <u>Southwestern Journals of Adolph F. Bandelier, Vol. II, 1883-1884</u>. Charles H. Lange and Carroll L. Riley, eds. Albuquerque: UNM Press and SAR, 1970.

32. BANDELIER, ADOLPH A.: <u>A History of the Southwest</u>. Vol. 1 of 5 volumes to be published. Ernest J. Burrus, S. J., ed. St. Louis: Jesuit Historical Institute, 1969.
Studies prepared in the 1890's for Pope Leo XIII. When complete, these volumes will provide first-hand data of the highest order.

33. CLARK, ANN NOLAN and FRANCES CAREY: <u>A Child's Story of New Mexico</u>. New York: University Publishing Co., 1941.

34. FERGUSSON, ERNA: <u>New Mexico, a Pageant of Three Peoples</u>. New York: Alfred A. Knopf, 1951. Revised Edition.
Portrayal of Indian, Hispanic and Anglo cultures in New Mexico from past to present.

35. HAMMOND, GEORGE P. and THOMAS C. DONNELLY: <u>The Story of New Mexico</u>. Albuquerque: UNM Press, 1936.
Highly readable and well-documented historical overview.

36. HARPER, ALLAN G., KALERVO OBERG and ANDREW CORDOVA: Man and Resources in the Middle Rio Grande Valley. Albuquerque: UNM Press, 1943.
The single best volume on the historical development of Spanish-speaking communities of northern New Mexico.

37. HORGAN, PAUL: The Great River. New York: Rhinehart, 1954.
Readable saga of New Mexico history, short on references.

38. JOSEPHY, ALVIN M., JR.: The Indian Heritage of America. New York: Alfred A. Knopf, 1969.
History-archeology-ethnology-linguistics-sociology, with good photos and interesting, non-technical presentation, including New Mexico.

39. LOONEY, RALPH: Haunted Highways. New York: Hastings House, 1968.
Attractive combination of pictures and light history of old New Mexico towns. Maps.

40. REEVE, FRANK D.: New Mexico, A Short Illustrated History. Denver: Sage Books, 1964. Available in paperback.

E. PUEBLO CULTURE: DESCRIPTIVE, GENERAL

41. BANDELIER, ADOLPH A. and EDGAR L. HEWETT: Indians of the Rio Grande Valley. Albuquerque: UNM Press, 1937.

42. COLLIER, JOHN: On the Gleaming Way. Denver: Sage Books, 1962.
A new edition, sumptuously illustrated, of the best-known work by the Indian Commissioner of the New Deal era. Includes material on Navajos and Apaches, but more on Pueblos.

43. DORSEY, GEORGE A.: Indians of the Southwest. Chicago: George T. Nicholson Co. for the Atchison, Topeka and Santa Fe Railway Passenger Department, 1903.
An easygoing record of a journey in the early 20th century, with lively description of Indian communities visited.

44. DOZIER, EDWARD P.: Hano: A Tewa Indian Community in Arizona. New York, Chicago, etc.: Holt Rhinehart and Winston, Inc., 1966.
History and analytic description of the descendants of 1696 refugees from Spanish oppression of Rio Grande Pueblos.

45. DOZIER, EDWARD P.: The Pueblos Indians of North America. New York, Chicago, etc: Holt, Rhinehart and Winston, Inc., 1970.
Thorough study of Pueblo Indians from prehistoric times to the present, with special attention to effects of intercultural contact.

46. DUMAREST, FATHER NOEL: Notes on Cochiti, New Mexico. Menasha, Wisconsin: AAAM, Vol. 6, No. 3, 1919.
Classic Ethnographic description.

47. DUTTON, BERTHA P.: Let's Explore! Indian Villages, Past and Present: Santa Fe Area. Santa Fe: MNM Press. Revised Edition, 1971.
Popular description of archeological and current sites of Pueblo habitation in northcentral New Mexico.

48. EDDY, FRANK W.: Metates and Manos: Basic Corn Grinding Tools of the Southwest. Santa Fe: MNM Press. Popular Pamphlet series, 1964.

49. EGGAN, FRED: Social Organization of the Western Pueblos. Chicago: University of Chicago Press, 1931.
First-rate study of major theoretical importance.

50. GODDARD, PLINY E.: Indians of the Southwest. New York: AMNH Handbook Series No. 2, 1931.
Concise and easy-to-read introduction to tribes.

51. GOLDFRANK, ESTHER: "Socialization, Personality and the Structure of Pueblo Society". AA 47/4: 519-539, 1945.
Discussion of conflicting views of visiting anthropologists regarding Zuñis.

52. ORTIZ, ALFONSO: The Tewa World. Chicago: University of Chicago Press, 1969.
The best single structural analysis of Tewa (and ultimately all Pueblo) cultural design.

53. ORTIZ, ALFONSO, ed.: New Perspectives on the Pueblos. Albuquerque: UNM Press, 1972.
An important collection of discussion papers based on a 1969 symposium.

54. PARSONS, ELSIE CLEWS: "Notes on Acoma and Laguna". AA 20/2: 162-186, 1918.
A brief introduction to a neighboring pair of Keresan Pueblos.

55. PARSONS, ELSIE CLEWS: "Isleta, New Mexico". BAE Annual Report, 47: 193-466, 1932.

56. PARSONS, ELSIE CLEWS: Taos Pueblo. Santa Fe: Laboratory of Anthropology, General Series in Anthropology, No. 2, 1936.
Writings on Taos are limited. This is one of the few.

57. PARSONS, ELSIE CLEWS: "Picuris, New Mexico". AA 41/2: 206-222, 1939.
Description of daily life, religion, government, ceremonial calendar. An aged survivor of the Pueblo described the past.

58. PARSONS, ELSIE CLEWS: Pueblo Indian Religion. Chicago: University of Chicago Press, 1939.
2 vols. Excellent, comprehensive and comparative.

59. STUBBS, STANLEY A.: Bird's-Eye View of the Pueblos. Norman, Oklahoma: University of Oklahoma Press, 1950.
A good physical survey, with photographs, maps and town plans.

60. TALAYESVA, DON: Sun Chief: Autobiography of a Hopi. (Leo Simmons, ed.). New Haven: Yale University Press, 1942.
A sensitive personal account of life among the Hopis of northeastern Arizona.

61. VOGT, EVON Z.: "A Study of the Southwestern Fiesta System as Exemplified by the Laguna Fiesta". AA 57/4: 820-839, 1955.
Helpful for the understanding of Pueblo ritual and the influences of Catholicism.

62. WHITE, LESLIE A.: "The Acoma Indians". BAE Annual Report, 47: 17-192, 1932.
Thorough ethnography. White reported on 5 out of 7 Keresan Pueblos, as witnessed by the next 4 titles.

63. WHITE, LESLIE A.: The Pueblo of San Felipe. AAAM No. 38, 1932.

64. WHITE, LESLIE A.: The Pueblo of Santo Domingo. AAAM No. 43, 1935.

65. WHITE, LESLIE A.: The Pueblo of Santa Ana. AAAM No. 60, 1942.

66. WHITE, LESLIE A.: The Pueblo of Sia, New Mexico. BAE Bulletin No. 184, 1962.

F. NAVAJO AND APACHE: DESCRIPTIVE, GENERAL

67. BAILEY, FLORA L.: "Navajo Motor Habits". AA 44/2: 210-234, 1942.
Observations on a distinctive Navajo way of moving through everyday activities, such as sitting, walking, eating, shearing sheep, carding wool, spinning, etc.

68. CARR, MALCOLM, KATHERINE SPENCER and DORIANE WOOLLEY: "Navajo Clans and Marriage at Pueblo Alto". AA 41/2: 245-257, 1939.
Analysis of family-clan tier of 888 individuals and 247 marriages. Seven of the 39 named clans in the Pueblo Alto area were missing in the study population.

69. DYK, WALTER: Son of Old Man Hat. New York: Harcourt Brace, 1938.
Autobiography of a Navajo born during the return from captivity at the Bosque Redondo in 1868. His childhood and youth are portrayed as he experienced them.

70. GOODWIN, GRENVILLE: "The Characteristics and Function of Clans in Southern Athapaskan Culture". AA 39/3: 394-407, 1937.
Comparison of Navajo with various Apache kinship systems and these, in turn, with Pueblo clans.

71. HILL, W.W.: "The Status of the Hermaphrodite and Transvestite in Navajo Culture". AA 37/2: 273-279, 1935.
Hermaphrodites and transvestites have the reputation of possessing special powers, including those of witchcraft.

72. HILL, W.W.: Navajo Warfare. New Haven: Yale University Publications in Anthropology, No. 5, 1936.
Recollections of the last surviving Navajo warriors.

73. HILL, W.W.: The Agricultural and Hunting Methods of the Navajo Indians. New Haven: Yale University Publications in Anthropology, No. 18, 1938.

74. HILL, W.W.: Navajo Salt Gathering. Albuquerque: UNM Anthropological Series, Bulletin 3/4, 1940.

75. KAUT, CHARLES: "Western Apache Clan and Phratry Organization". AA 58/1: 140-146, 1956.
Synthesis, based on field research and Goodwin's studies.

76. KLUCKHOHN, CLYDE: Navaho Witchcraft. Cambridge: PPMAAE 22/2, 1944.
The pervasive belief in witchcraft has, during times of social upheaval, exerted a powerful influence on events.

77. KLUCKHOHN, CLYDE and DOROTHEA LEIGHTON: The Navaho. Cambridge: Harvard University Press, 1951.
Basic Navajo ethnography, well documented.

78. KLUCKHOHN, CLYDE, W.W. HILL and LUCY WALES KLUCKHOHN: Navaho Material Culture. Cambridge: The Belknap Press of Harvard University Press, 1971.
An exhaustive inventory from many sources.

79. KLUCKHOHN, CLYDE, ALEXANDER H. LEIGHTON and DOROTHEA C. LEIGHTON: The Navaho Door. Cambridge: Harvard University Press, 1944.
A psychologically oriented account of the Navajo, with a section of Navajo life stories.

80. LEVY, JEROLD E.: "The Fate of Navajo Twins". AA 66/4: 883-887, 1964.
Ambivalent attitudes toward twin births affect survival rates.

81. MORGAN, WILLIAM: Human Wolves Among the Navajo. New Haven: Yale University Publications in Anthropology, No. 11, 1936.
A special form of witchcraft belief described by a Navajo author.

82. NEWCOMB, FRANC J.: "Navajo Calendar". New Mexico Magazine 18/1: 18-19, 32-34, 1940.
A brief, popular account of how Navajos reckon the passage of time.

83. MATSON, DANIEL S. and ALBERT H. SCHROEDER, trans. and ed.: "Cordero's Description of the Apache 1796". NMHR 32/4: 335-356, 1957. First-hand observation of the various divisions of Apaches and Navajos in the late 18th century.

84. OPLER, MORRIS E. "The Kinship Systems of the Southern Athapaskan Speaking Tribes". AA 38/4: 620-633, 1936.
A comparative work. Moiety and clan were supposedly borrowed from the Eastern and Western Pueblos respectively.

85. OPLER, MORRIS E. "A Summary of Jicarilla Apache Culture". AA 38/2: 202-233, 1936.
An abbreviated ethnography, but the best available on the Jicarilla.

86. OPLER, MORRIS E. An Apache Life-Way: The Economic, Social and Religious Institutions of the Chiricahua Indians. Chicago: University of Chicago Press, 1941.
Thorough ethnography, with historical background included.

87. REED, ERIK K.: "Information on the Navaho in 1706". AA 43/3: 485-487, 1941.
A brief communication summarizing what was known of the Navajos as a distinctive group during a period when they were usually lumped with the Apaches.

88. REICHARD, GLADYS: Navajo Religion. New York, The Bollingen Foundation Series (2 Vols.), 1950.
The most complete study available on Navajo religious philosophy and practice.

89. YOUNG, ROBERT W.: The Role of the Navajo in the Southwestern Drama. Gallup: Gallup Independent, 1968.
Readable, with especially good coverage of early times.

G. TOPOGRAPHY, TRAVEL, MINERAL RESOURCES AND MINING

90. ARROWSMITH, REX, ed.: Mines of the Old Southwest. Santa Fe: Stagecoach Press, 1963.
Early reports on the mines of New Mexico and Arizona by explorers.

91. BUNTING, BAINBRIDGE: "Take a Trip with NMA". New Mexico Architect, 12/9 and 10, 1970.
The entire October issue of the magazine is devoted to a series of trips through towns and villages of northern New Mexico, written by a professor of architecture. Excellent photos of buildings and art works, some in color.

92. CROSNO, MAUDE D. and MASTERS CROSNO: Discovering New Mexico. Austin, Texas: The Steck Co., 1950.
Prepared for juvenile readers.

93. HARRINGTON, JOHN P.: The Ethnogeography of the Tewa Indians. BAE 29th Annual Report (Extract), 1916.
A monumental work on Tewa place names, for serious scholars.

94. JONES, FAYETTE: Old Mines and Ghost Camps of New Mexico. Fort Davis, Texas: Frontier Book Co., 1968.

95. LEWIS, MARVIN, ed.: The Mining Frontier: Contemporary Accounts from the American West in the 19th Century. Norman: University of Oklahoma Press, 1968.

96. McKENNA, JAMES A.: Black Range Tales, New York: Wilson-Erickson, 1936.
Personal reminiscences of early mining days in the Hillsboro-Kingston-Silver City area.

97. NORTHROP, S. A.: Minerals of New Mexico. Albuquerque: UNM Press, 1959.

98. NORTHROP, S. A.: "New Mexico's Fossil Record". NM Quarterly 32/1 and 2, with supplement of 75 pages, 1962.
The authoritative source for information on fossils.

99. PEARCE, THOMAS M., ed.: New Mexico Place Names, A Geographical Dictionary. Albuquerque: UNM Press, 1965.

100-107. SCENIC TRIPS TO THE GEOLOGIC PAST
Socorro, New Mexico: State Bureau of Mines and Mineral Resources. This pamphlet series provides valuable topographical and geological information to the interested traveler. Titles of the individual pamphlets, as listed below, define the coverage of each:

100. <u>Santa Fe, New Mexico</u>. Pamphlet No. 1, by Brewster Baldwin and Frank Kottlowski, 1955.

101. <u>Taos-Red River-Eagle Nest, New Mexico Circle Drive</u>. Pamphlet No. 2, by John H. Schilling, 1956.

102. <u>Roswell-Capitan-Ruidoso and Bottomless Lakes Park, New Mexico</u>. Pamphlet No. 3, by John E. Allen and Frank E. Kottlowski, 1958.

103. <u>Southern Zuñi Mountains</u>. Pamphlet No. 4, by Roy W. Foster, 1958.

104. <u>Silver City-Santa Rita-Hurley, New Mexico</u>. Pamphlet No. 5, by John H. Schilling, 1959.

105. <u>Trail Guide to the Upper Pecos</u>. Pamphlet No. 6, by Arthur Montgomery and Patrick Sutherland, 1960.

106. <u>High Plains: Northeastern New Mexico Raton-Capulin Mountain-Clayton</u>. Pamphlet No. 7 by William Muehlberger et al, 1961.

107. <u>Mosaic of New Mexico's Scenery, Rocks and History</u>. Pamphlet No. 8, by Paige W. Christiansen and Frank E. Kottlowski, 1967.

108. SULLY, JOHN M.: "The Story of the Santa Rita Cooper Mine". <u>Old Santa Fe 3/3: 133-149, 1916</u>. Mining in southwestern New Mexico from Colonial times.

109. UNITED STATES GEOLOGICAL SURVEY: <u>Mineral and Water Resources of New Mexico</u>. Socorro: State Bureau of Mines and Mineral Resources, Bull. No. 87, 1965.

II. ARCHEOLOGY

A. PALEO-INDIANS AND ARCHAIC DESERT GATHERERS

110. AGOGINO, GEORGE A. and JAMES HESTER: "The Santa Ana Pre-Ceramic Sites". El Palacio 60/4: 131-140, 1953.
Remains of a pre-Pueblo culture 3-6,000 years old on Santa Ana Pueblo lands.

111. BRYAN, KIRK and JOSEPH H. TOULOUSE, JR.: "The San Jose Non-Ceramic Culture and its Relation to a Puebloan Culture in New Mexico". American Antiquity 8/3:269-280, 1943.

112. CAMPBELL, JOHN M. and FLORENCE H. ELLIS: "The Atrisco Sites: Cochise Manifestations in the Middle Rio Grande Valley". American Antiquity 17/3: 211-221, 1952.
A group of hunter-gatherers occupied sites south of Albuquerque, from about 3,000 to 500 B.C.

113. COOK, HAROLD J.: "Glacial Age Man in New Mexico". Scientific American 139: 38-40, 1928. Early report on Folsom Man.

114. DICK, HERBERT: Bat Cave. SAR, Monograph No. 27, 1965.
Report on the site in southwestern New Mexico which yielded samples of maize, pod corn and squash dated 4,000 to 2,000 B.C. Evidence of the earliest northward spread of Middle American agriculture.

115. HIBBEN, FRANK C.: "Sandia Man: Artifacts Found in Basal Layers of a Cave". Scientific American 163: 14-15, 1940.
An early report on the earliest dated Paleo-Indian find.

116. HIBBEN, FRANK C.: Evidences of Early Occupation in Sandia Cave, New Mexico and Other Sites in the Sandia-Manzano Region. Smithsonian Misc. Coll. No. 99/23. Washington, D.C.: GPO, 1941.
Detailed technical report on the Sandia finds.

117. HIBBEN, FRANK C.: "Sites of the Paleo-Indian in the Middle Rio Grande Valley". American Antiquity 17/1: 41-46, 1951.
Sites in the vicinity of Albuquerque, Tome and Rio Puerco combine bones of extinct mammals with scraping-chopping implements, milling stones and hearth sites, characteristic of Archaic Desert culture.

118. JENNINGS, JESSE D.: "The Desert West" in *Prehistoric Man in the New World*, J. D. Jennings and E. Norbeck, eds.: 149-174. Chicago: University of Chicago Press, 1964.
Excellent recent summary article of Paleo-Indian and Archaic Desert cultures.

119. KRIEGER, ALEX D.: "Early Man in the New World" in *Prehistoric Man in the New World*, J. D. Jennings and E. Norbeck, eds.: 23-81. Chicago: University of Chicago Press, 1964.
Pioneer synthesis on "pre-projectile" sites throughout the New World, antedating Paleo-Indian culture, and definition of early cultural stages, extending back as far as 40,000 years. Some sites are in New Mexico.

120. SAMPLE, L. L. and A. MOHR: "Some Pre-Ceramic Sites Near Farmington, New Mexico". *The Masterkey 34/4: 128-146, 1960*.

121. SELLERS, E. H.: *Early Man in America: A Study in Prehistory*. Austin: University of Texas Press, 1952.

122. WORMINGTON, H. M.: *Ancient Man in North America*. Denver Museum of Natural History, Popular Science Series No. 4 (Third Edition, Revised), 1950.
The best overview of the continent as a whole with good, but not the most recent, coverage of the Southwest.

123. WORMINGTON, H. M.: *Prehistoric Indians of the Southwest*. Denver Museum of Natural History, Popular Series No. 7 (Fourth Printing), 1959.
Highly readable and well documented, though not the latest.

B. ANASAZI-PUEBLO

124. AMSDEN, CHARLES A.: *Prehistoric Southwesterners from Basketmaker to Pueblo*. Los Angeles: Southwest Museum, 1949.

125. BANDELIER, ADOLPH A.: *The Delight Makers*. New York: Dodd, Mead and Company, 1890.
Novelistic treatment of the life and activities of Pueblo people before the coming of the white man. A classic.

126. BRAND, D. D., F. M. HAWLEY and F. C. HIBBEN: <u>Tseh So, a Small House Ruin in Chaco Canyon, New Mexico</u>. Albuquerque: UNM Anthropological Series, Bull. No. 2/2, 1937.

127. BULLARD, W. R., JR.: <u>The Cerro Colorado Site and Pithouse Architecture in the Southwestern United States</u>. PPMAAE 44/2, 1962.
Technical, but an important work on the development of the southwestern pithouse, prior to 900 A.D.

128. EDDY, FRANK W.: <u>Excavations at Los Pinos Phase Sites in the Navajo Reservoir District</u>. Santa Fe: MNM Papers in Anthropology, No. 4, 1961.
Description and discussion of Basketmaker II villages in northwestern New Mexico.

129. EDDY, FRANK W.: <u>Prehistory in the Navajo Reservoir District, Northwestern New Mexico</u>. Santa Fe: MNM Papers in Anthropology, No. 15/1 and 2, 1966.
A major synthesis covering 8 years of study of prehistoric and early historic settlements in northwestern New Mexico.

130. ELLIS, FLORENCE H.: "Jemez Kiva Magic". <u>SWJA 8/2: 147-163, 1952</u>.
Explanation of possible functions of the pits and holes often found in prehistoric Pueblo ceremonial chambers.

131. ELLIS, FLORENCE H.: "Archeological History of Nambe Pueblo 14th Century to Present". <u>American Antiquity 39/4: 34-42, 1964</u>.
Surveys and test excavations in and around Nambe are coupled with informant data to trace the local movements of this Pueblo group.

132. ELLIS, FLORENCE H.: "The Immediate History of Zia Pueblo as Derived from Excavation in Refuse Deposits". <u>American Antiquity 31/6: 806-811, 1966</u>. Brief review of field data.

133. ELLIS, FLORENCE H.: "Where Did the Pueblo People Come From?" <u>El Palacio 74/3: 35-43, 1967</u>.
Attempt to link tradition with archeological and linguistic evidence. The results are debatable but intriguing.

134. ELLIS, FLORENCE H. and J. J. BRODY: "Ceramic Stratigraphy and Tribal History at Taos Pueblo". *American Antiquity* 29/3: 316-327, 1964.
Results of excavation of the refuse piles of Taos.

135. FERDON, EDWARD N., JR.: *A Trial Survey of Mexican-Southwestern Architectural Parallels.* Santa Fe: SAR Monograph, No. 21, 1955.
Discusses unique prehistoric architectural forms (tower kivas, multi-walled kivas, columned structures) in the Southwest and how they may be due to influences from Mexico.

136. GLADWIN, H.S.: *The Chaco Branch: Excavations at White Mound and the Red Mesa Valley.* Globe, Arizona: Medallion Papers, No. 33, 1945.
Sometimes controversial, but an important discussion of prehistoric Anasazi in the Chaco Canyon and Puerco River areas of western New Mexico.

137. GREEN, R.C.: "The Hormigas Site of the Largo-Gallina Phase". *El Palacio* 69/3: 142-157, 1962.
Good for its bibliography of the important books and articles on the Largo-Gallina Phase.

138. HALL, EDWARD T., JR.: *Early Stockaded Settlements in the Governador, New Mexico: A Marginal Anasazi Development from Basketmaker III to Pueblo I Times.* New York: Columbia University Studies in Archeology and Ethnology 2/1, 1944.
Technical but important.

139. HAMMACK, LAURENS C.: *Archeology of the Ute Dam and Reservoir, Northeastern New Mexico.* Santa Fe: MNM Papers in Anthropology, No. 14, 1965.
Important work on a little-studied area.

140. HAWLEY, FLORENCE (ELLIS): "Big Kivas, Little Kivas and Moiety Houses in Historical Reconstruction". *SWJA* 6/3: 286-302, 1950.
Relation of structures to social organization.

141. HEWETT, EDGAR L.: *The Chaco Canyon and its Monuments.* Albuquerque: UNM Press, 1936.
Highly readable summary with illustrations of most of the major ruins in the Chaco Canyon.

142. HEWETT, EDGAR L.: Pajarito Plateau and its Ancient People. Albuquerque: UNM Press, 1938.
Highly readable, well illustrated, regional coverage of archeology blended with ethnography.

143. HEWETT, EDGAR L. and BERTHA P. DUTTON: The Pueblo Indian World. Albuquerque: UNM-SAR, 1945.
Studies on the natural history of the Rio Grande Valley in relation to Pueblo Indian culture. Ecological approach, readable and profusely illustrated with photos and maps.

144. HIBBEN, FRANK C.: Excavation of the Riana Ruin and Chama Valley Survey. Albuquerque: UNM Anthropological Series, Bull. No. 2/1, 1937.
Primarily descriptive, but interprets prehistoric Pueblo occupation of the Chama Valley.

145. HIBBEN, FRANK C.: "Prehispanic Paintings at Pottery Mound". Archeology 13/4: 267-274, 1960.
Analysis of the splendid kiva murals at a ruin south of Albuquerque.

146. JEANCON, JEAN A.: Excavations in the Chama Valley, New Mexico. BAE Bull. No. 81, 1923.
One of the few research reports on this area.

147. JEANCON, JEAN A.: Archeological Investigations in the Taos Valley, New Mexico. Smithsonian Misc. Coll. 81/12, 1929.
Mainly descriptive.

148. JUDD, NEIL M.: The Material Culture of Pueblo Bonito. Smithsonian Misc. Coll. 124, 1954.
Excellent illustrations and description of the contents of this major site.

149. KIDDER, ALFRED V.: The Artifacts of Pecos. Andover: Phillips Academy and the Carnegie Institution, 1932.
A standard reference book for scholars of the Southwest.

150. KIDDER, ALFRED V.: Pecos Pueblo: Archeological Notes. PPMAAE Vol. 5, 1958.
Description of the architecture of the pueblo and interpretation.

151. KLUCKHOHN, CLYDE, PAUL REITER ET AL: Preliminary Report on the 1937 Excavations at Bc 50-51, Chaco Canyon. Albuquerque: UNM Anthropological Series, Bull. 3/2, 1939.
A model archeological monograph with ample description and comments. Brand, Hawley and Hibben, 1937 is a continuation of reporting on this excavation.

152. LAMBERT, MARJORIE F.: Paa-ko, a Chronicle of an Indian Village in North Central New Mexico. SAR Monograph No. 19, 1954.
An outstanding archeological report for serious readers.

153. McNUTT, C. H.: Early Puebloan Occupations at Tesuque By-Pass and in the Upper Rio Grande Valley. Ann Arbor: Anthropological Papers of the University of Michigan Museum of Anthropology, No. 40, 1969.
Describes and discusses Pueblo I-II development in the area just north of Santa Fe.

154. MERA, HARRY P.: Ceramic Clues to the Prehistory of North-Central New Mexico. Santa Fe: Laboratory of Anthropology Technical Series, Bull. No. 8, 1935.

155. MORRIS, EARL H.: The Aztec Ruin. AMNH Anthropological Papers, Vol. 26/1, 1919.
Primarily descriptive, but the main work on this important site.

156. MORRIS, EARL H.: "The Beginnings of Pottery Making in the San Juan Area: Unfired Prototypes and the Wares of the Earliest Ceramic Period". AMNH Anthropological Papers, Vol. 28: 125-198, 1927.
Very good documentation of prehistoric transition.

157. MORRIS, EARL H.: Archeological Studies in the La Plata District: Southwestern Colorado and Northwestern New Mexico. Carnegie Institution Publ. No. 533, 1939.
Description and synthesis dealing with the non-cliff-dwelling sites of the Classic Mesa Verde Pueblos and their antecedents.

158. MORRIS, EARL H. and ROBERT F. BURGH: Anasazi Basketry. Carnegie Institution Publ. No. 533, 1941.
Covers Basketmaker II-III in the San Juan Basin.

159. NELSON, NELS C.: Pueblo Ruins of the Galisteo Basin.
AMNH Anthropological Papers, Vol. 15/1, 1914.
Good combination of archeology with popular history. Definitive study of a series of Southern Tanoan Pueblos.

160. OSBORNE, DOUGLAS: "Solving the Riddles of Wetherill Mesa." National Geographic 125: 155-195, 1964.
Popular article on recent excavations in Mesa Verde country.

161. PECKHAM, STEWART: "Three Pithouse Sites Near Albuquerque". New Mexico Highway Salvage Archeology, Vol. III: 39-70, 1957.
Succinct description of Basketmaker III-Pueblo I sites and artifacts.

162. REED, ERIK K.: "The Distinctive Features and Distribution of the San Juan Anasazi Culture". SWJA 2/3: 295-305, 1946.
Synthesis.

163. REED, ERIK K.: "The Western Pueblo Archeological Complex". El Palacio 55/1: 9-15, 1948.
Synthesis.

164. REED, ERIK K. "Types of Village Plan Layouts in the Southwest". Viking Fund Publications in Anthropology 23:11-17, 1956.
Synthesis.

165. REED, ERIK K.: "The Greater Southwest" in Prehistoric Man in the New World, J. D. Jennings and E. Norbeck, eds.: 175-191. Chicago: University of Chicago Press, 1964.
An important recent work of area-wide synthesis.

166. ROBERTS, FRANK H. H., JR.: Shabik'eschee Village: A Late Basketmaker Site in the Chaco Canyon, New Mexico. BAE Bulletin No. 92, 1928.
Descriptive, an early study of Basketmaker III.

167. RUPPE, R.J.: "The Archeological Survey: A Defense". American Antiquity 31/3: 313-333, 1966.
Summary of the archeology of the Acoma area.

168. SCHOENWETTER, J. and FRANK W. EDDY: Alluvial and Palynological Reconstruction of Environments: Navajo Reservoir District. Santa Fe: MNM Papers in Anthropology No. 13, 1964.
An application of natural sciences in the inference of prehistoric environment as it may have influenced Pueblo people in northwestern New Mexico.

169. SCHOENWETTER, J. and ALFRED DITTERT, JR.: "An Ecological Interpretation of Anasazi Settlement Patterns" in *Anthropological Archeology in the Americas: 41-66.* Washington, D.C.: The Anthropological Society of Washington, 1968.
Paleoecology: changes in settlement patterns correlated with environmental changes on the Colorado Plateau. Good bibliography.

170. SMITH, W., R. B. WOODBURY and N. F. S. WOODBURY: *The Excavation of Hawikuh by Frederick Webb Hodge.* Contributions from the Museum of the American Indian, Heye Foundation, Vol. 50, 1966.
Final report on the excavation of this important Zuñi village, visited by Coronado in 1540.

171. STUBBS, STANLEY A.: "Summary Report on an Early Pueblo Site in the Tesuque Valley, New Mexico". *El Palacio 61/2: 43-45, 1954.*
Description and discussion of a pit house, pueblo site and Great Kiva in the Santa Fe area, dated 1000-1150 A.D.

172. STUBBS, STANLEY and W. S. STALLINGS, JR.: *Excavations at Pindi Pueblo, New Mexico.* Santa Fe: SAR Monograph No. 18, 1957.
The only comprehensive report on archeology of the Santa Fe area.

173. TICHY, MARJORIE F. (LAMBERT): "The Archeology of Puaray". *El Palacio 46/7: 145-165, 1939.*

174. TOULOUSE, JOSEPH H., JR. and R. L. STEPHENSON: *Excavations at Pueblo Pardo, Central New Mexico.* Santa Fe: MNM Papers in Anthropology, No. 2, 1960.
Primarily, the description of a Pueblo III-IV village near Gran Quivira.

175. VIVIAN, R. GORDON: *The Hubbard Site and Other Tri-Wall Structures in New Mexico and Colorado.* National Park Service: Archeological Research Series, No. 5, 1959.
Description and commentary on some unusual architectural forms in the Chaco Canyon and Mesa Verde areas.

176. VIVIAN, R. GORDON: *Gran Quivira: Excavations at a 17th Century Jumano Pueblo.* National Park Service: Archeological Research Series, No. 8, 1965.
Current thoughts on occupants of large prehistoric and early historic pueblos in central New Mexico.

177. VIVIAN, R. GORDON and PAUL REITER: The Great Kivas of Chaco Canyon and Their Relationships. Santa Fe: SAR Monograph No. 22, 1960.
A synthesis dealing with the huge ceremonial structures of the Anasazi area.

178. VIVIAN, R. GORDON and TOM W. MATHEWS: Kin Kletso, a Pueblo III Community in Chaco Canyon, New Mexico. Southwestern Monuments Association: Technical Series, Vol. 6/1, 1964.
One of the best summaries of Chaco Canyon archeology.

179. VIVIAN, R. GWINN and N. W. CLENDENEN: "The Denison Site: Four Pit Houses Near Isleta, New Mexico". El Palacio 72/2: 5-26, 1963.
Summarizes current knowledge of the Pueblo people in the Middle Rio Grande in the 9th-11th Centuries.

180. WENDORF, FRED (COMPILER): Salvage Archeology in the Chama Valley, New Mexico. Santa Fe: SAR Monograph No. 17, 1953.
Description and comments concerning two Pueblo III-IV sites of this upper Rio Grande tributary.

181. WENDORF, FRED: "The Archeology of Northeastern New Mexico", El Palacio 67/1: 2-12, 1960.
A synthesis of available data on a little-known but important part of New Mexico.

182. WENDORF, FRED and ERIK K. REED: "An Alternative Reconstruction of Northern Rio Grande Prehistory". El Palacio 42: 131-173, 1955.
Speculative synthesis on a controversial topic.   See Ellis (133).

183. WETHERINGTON, RONALD K.: Excavations at Pot Creek Pueblo. Taos, New Mexico: Fort Burgwin Research Center, Publ. No. 6, 1968.
Description and interpretation of a major ruin in a peripheral Pueblo area, the northern Rio Grande.

C. MOGOLLON-HOHOKAM

184. BRADFIELD, WESLEY: Cameron Creek Village. Santa Fe: SAR, 1929.
An important source on the Mogollon area.

185. COSGROVE, H. S. and C. B.: *The Swarts Ruin: A Typical Mimbres Site in Southwestern New Mexico.* PPMAAE Vol. 15/1, 1952.
The best described and illustrated of all Mimbres sites. Many drawings and photos of the distinctive Mimbres pottery.

186. HAURY, EMIL W.: "The Hohokam, First Masters of the American Desert". *National Geographic 131/5: 670-695, 1967.*
Exciting new discovery of early irrigation techniques in the Lower Gila Valley.

187. JELINEK, A. J.: *A Prehistoric Sequence in the Middle Pecos Valley.* Ann Arbor: Anthropological Papers of the University of Michigan Museum of Anthropology, No. 31, 1967.
Technical, but just about all there is on this peripheral southwestern area.

188. LAMBERT, MARJORIE and J. RICHARD AMBLER: *A Survey and Excavation of Caves in Hidalgo County, New Mexico.* Santa Fe: SAR Monograph No. 25, 1961.
More on the Mogollon area.

189. LEHMER, DONALD J.: *The Jornada Branch of the Mogollon.* University of Arizona, Social Science Bulletin No. 17, 1948.
A description and synthesis of a variant of the Mogollon culture in southern New Mexico.

190. MARTIN, PAUL S.: *Digging Into History.* Chicago: Natural History Museum Popular Series No. 38, 1959.
A good, popular summary of Mogollon archeology.

191. MARTIN, PAUL S. and J. B. RINALDO: *Sites of the Reserve Phase, Pine Lawn Valley, Western New Mexico.* Chicago: Field Museum of Natural History, Fieldiana: Anthropology, Vol. 38/3, 1950.
Describes and discusses the earliest masonry dwellings (circa A.D. 1000) of the Mogollon culture in this area.

192. MARTIN, P. S., J. B. RINALDO, E. BLUHM, H. CULTLER and R. GRANGE, JR.: *Mogollon Cultural Continuity and Change: The Stratigraphic Analysis of Tularosa and Cordova Caves.* Chicago: Field Museum of Natural History, Fieldiana: Anthropology, Vol. 40, 1952.
Contents of two caves yielding much perishable material remains of the Cochise and Mogollon cultures.

193. MARTIN, P. S., J. B. RINALDO, E. BLUHM and H. CUTLER: Higgins Flat Pueblo, Western New Mexico. Chicago: Field Museum of Natural History, Fieldiana: Anthropology, No. 45, 1956.
A major late (Tularosa Phase, A.D. 1150-1250) village near Reserve, New Mexico. Primarily descriptive.

194. MARTIN, P. S., J. B. RINALDO and E. R. BARTER: Late Mogollon Communities: Four Sites of the Tularosa Phase, Western New Mexico. Chicago: Field Museum of Natural History, Fieldiana: Anthropology, Vol. 49/1, 1957.
Describes and comments on the sites of the last Mogollon occupants of the area around Reserve, New Mexico.

195. McCLUNEY, EUGENE: "The Hatchet Site: A Preliminary Report". Southwestern Lore 26/4: 70-73, 1961.
A location near Three Rivers, southeastern New Mexico, considered to be Mogollon.

196. MERA, HARRY P.: An Outline of the Ceramic Development in Southern and Southeastern New Mexico. Santa Fe: Laboratory of Anthropology Technical Series. Bulletin No. 11, 1943.
Technical, but covers the Eastern Mogollon Culture variant, just defined in 1943.

197. PECKHAM, STEWART: "Hillside Pueblo: Early Masonry Architecture in the Reserve Area, New Mexico". El Palacio 65/3: 81-94, 1958.
Description and synthesis.

198. PECKHAM, STEWART, FRED WENDORF and E. N. FERDON: "Excavation Near Apache Creek, New Mexico" in Highway Salvage Archeology, Vol. 2/8: 17-86, 1956.
Mogollon pithouses or pithouse kivas, from about A.D. 500 to 1150.

199. PESO, CHARLES DI: "Casas Grandes and the Gran Chichimeca". El Palacio 75/4: 47-61, 1968.
Influence of higher cultures of Mesoamerica upon the outlying northern regions of Arizona and New Mexico through the mediation of traders (puchteca).

200. WHEAT, JOE BEN: The Mogollon Culture Prior to A.D. 1000. Society for American Archeology Memoir No. 10 (also AAAM No. 82), 1955.

D. NAVAJO-APACHE

201. FARMER, MALCOLM A.: "Navajo Archeology of the Upper Blanco and Largo Canyons, Northern New Mexico". American Antiquity 8/1: 65-79, 1942.
Inventory of Dinetah sites and their contents and synthesis on early Navajo-Pueblo relations.

202. GUNNERSON, DOLORES A.: "The Southern Athabascans: Their Arrival in the Southwest". El Palacio 63/11-12: 346-365, 1956.

203. GUNNERSON, DOLORES A.: "Man and Bison on the Plains in the Prehistoric Record". Plains Anthropologist 17/55: 1-10, 1972.
Archeological and documentary evidence for vast increase of buffalo herds on the Southern Plains before 1541, barring settlement by farm villagers but attracting Apache hunters with movable skin tents, pack dogs and prior experience with large-herd animals of the far north.

204. GUNNERSON, JAMES H. "Apache Archeology in Northeastern New Mexico". American Antiquity 34/1: 32-39, 1969.

205. HALL, EDWARD T., JR.: "Recent Clues to the Athabascan Prehistory in the Southwest". AA 46/1: 98-105, 1944.
Relations between Rosa, Largo and Gallina phases of New Mexico prehistory and possible connection with arrival of Navajo.

206. KEUR, DOROTHY L.: Big Bead Mesa, an Archeological Study of Navaho Acculturation, 1745-1812. Memoirs of the Society for American Archeology, No. 1, 1941.
Early historic settlements at the southeastern margin of Dinetah, the traditional Navajo homeland.

207. KEUR, DOROTHY L.: "A Chapter in Navaho-Pueblo Relations". American Antiquity 10/1: 75-86, 1944.
In canyons of the San Juan drainage hogan remains were found in association with small pueblo-like structures, including towers, dated 1670-1770, remains of joint Navajo-Pueblo occupancy when Pueblos resisted Spanish domination.

208. RILEY, CARROLL L.: "A Survey of Navajo Archeology". University of Colorado Studies, Series in Anthropology No. 4: 45-60, 1954.
Brief overview.

E. UTE-COMANCHE

209. LISTER, ROBERT H. and HERBERT W. DICK: "Archeology of the Glade Park Area, a Progress Report". Southwestern Lore 17/4: 69-92, 1952.
Around 1150 A.D. "a pattern exhibiting conical-based paddle and anvil pottery, lateral and base-notched points, cave shelters and round brush huts, suggestive of historic Shoshonean culture" appeared over a wide area, replacing Pueblo-II culture in Utah, Arizona Strip, western Colorado, southern Nevada and southern California.

210. SCHROEDER, ALBERT A.: "Statement on the Early History and Archeology of the Gunnison River Basin". Southwestern Lore 19/3: 3-10, 1953.
Arrival of the Utes in the Southwest.

F. HISPANO

211. HAYES, ALDEN: "The Missing Convento of San Isidro". El Palacio 75/4: 35-40, 1968.
Ruins of a 17th century mission at the Pueblo de las Humanas (Gran Quivira), the southernmost Saline Pueblo (see Vivian, 1965).

212. STUBBS, STANLEY and BRUCE ELLIS: Chapel of San Miguel. Santa Fe: MNM Press. Museum Guide Series, No. 21, n.d.

213. TOULOUSE, JOSEPH H. JR.: The Mission of San Gregorio de Abó. Santa Fe: SAR Monograph No. 13, 1949.
Archeological study of the early Indian-Spanish contact period, with much architectural information.

III. SPANISH COLONIAL AND MEXICAN PERIODS (1540-1846)

A. EXPLORATION BY SPANIARDS: FIRST ENCOUNTERS WITH INDIANS.

214. BOLTON, HERBERT E.: Coronado, Knight of Pueblos and Plains. New York: Whittlesey House, 1949.

215. CASTANEDA, PEDRO DE: *The Journey of Coronado, 1540-1542*. Translated and edited by George Parker Winship. New York: A. S. Barnes and Co., 1904.
Recollections of one of Coronado's followers.

216. GIBSON, CHARLES: *Tlaxcala in the 16th Century*. New Haven: Yale University Press, 1952.
The regulations and inducements which brought contingents of Mexican Indians to New Mexico with each exploration party and with Oñate's settlers.

217. HAMMOND, GEORGE P. and AGAPITO REY: *The Rediscovery of New Mexico, 1580-1594*. Albuquerque: UNM Press, 1966.
Explorations of Chamuscado, Espejo, Castaño de Sosa, Morlete, Leyva de Bonilla and Humaña. Supersedes previous publications.

218. HEWETT, EDGAR L.: *Pre-hispanic Frescoes in the Rio Grande Valley*. Santa Fe: SAR Papers, n.s., No. 27, 1938.
Description of 1598 visit to Puaray by Oñate's men in Captain Gaspar Perez de Villagra's rhymed *Historia de la Nuevo Mexico* (1610) recorded information on the killing of the priests from the Rodriguez-Chamuscado expedition, depicted in kiva murals.

219. JONES, OAKAH L.: *Pueblo Warriors and Spanish Conquest*. Norman: University of Oklahoma Press, 1966.
Confrontation of distinct ways of life in the period of exploration and conquest.

220. SCHROEDER, ALBERT H. "Shifting for Survival in the Spanish Southwest". *NMHR 40/3-4: 201-310, 1968*.
Movement of Pueblos in 16th, 17th and 18th centuries. Good map.

221. SCHROEDER, ALBERT H. and DAN S. MATSON: *A Colony on the Move: Gaspar Castaño de Sosa's Journal, 1590-1591*. Santa Fe: SAR, 1965.
The authors retrace de Sosa's route, adding interesting commentary to the translation of the journal.

222. SIMMONS, MARC: "Tlaxcalans in the Spanish Borderlands". *NMHR 39/2, 101-110, 1964*.
A companion piece to Gibson, 1952 traces evidence of the transition of Barrio Analco in Santa Fe from Tlaxcalan to Genizaro occupancy.

223. THOMAS, ALFRED B., ed.: <u>After Coronado</u>. Norman: University of Oklahoma Press, 1935.
Spanish exploration northeast of New Mexico, 1696-1727.

B. <u>INDIAN EXPERIENCE</u>

1. <u>PUEBLOS</u>

224. ADAMS, ELEANOR B.: "Fray Silvestre and the Obstinate Hopi". <u>NMHR 38/2: 97-138, 1963</u>.
Translation and commentary of a diary recording an unsuccessful mission in 1775. Good description of the Hopi Pueblos and their tactics of resistance to Spanish domination.

225. CHAVEZ, FRAY ANGELICO: "Pohe-Yemo's Representation and the Pueblo Revolt of 1680". <u>NMHR 42/2: 85-126, 1967</u>.
Speculative but documented hypothesis that the Pueblo Revolt was masterminded by the son of an African father and Mexican Indian mother.

226. DOZIER, EDWARD P.: "Spanish-Catholic Influences on Rio Grande Pueblo Religion". <u>AA 60/3: 441-448, 1958</u>.

227. ESPINOSA, J. MANUEL: <u>First Expedition of de Vargas into New Mexico, 1692</u>. Albuquerque: Coronado Historical Series, Vol. 10, 1940.
Records of de Vargas' encounters with Pueblos, both in battle and in negotiation.

228. HACKETT, C. W. and C. C. SHELBY: <u>Revolt of the Pueblo Indians and Otermin's Attempted Reconquest, 1680-1682</u>.
Albuquerque: Coronado Historical Series, Vols. 8-9, 1942. Reprinted 1970.
A major source, from primary documents.

229. HAWLEY, FLORENCE M.: "Pueblo Politics". <u>New Mexico Magazine 17/8: 16-17, 34-35, 1939</u>.
Explains difference between internal Pueblo government and the "elected" officials required by Spanish Colonial government.

230. HORGAN, PAUL: The Conquest of Santa Fe. New York: E. P. Dutton (paperback), 1956.
Readable history of Santa Fe.

231. HORGAN, PAUL: Conquistadors. Greenwich, Conn: Fawcett Publications, 1966. (Paperback, also a Spanish edition, available through Editorial Diana, S.A. Mexico, D.F.)
History of the Conquest of New Mexico.

232. KURATH, GERTRUDE P.: "Mexican Moriscas". Journal of American Folklore 62/244: 87-106, 1949. Analysis of the Matachine dance, introduced by the Spaniards to the Eastern Pueblos, during the process of conversion to Christianity.

233. SCHOLES, FRANCE V.: Troublous Times in New Mexico, 1659-1670. Albuquerque: Historical Society of New Mexico, Publications in History, Vol. 2, 1942.
Events leading to the Pueblo Revolt of 1680.

234. WALTER, PAUL A. F.: "Gran Quivira, One of the Cities That Died of Fear". El Palacio 5/14: 226-231, 1918.
Depopulation of Piro villages east of the Manzano Mountains due to Apache attacks in the 17th century.

235. WHITE, LESLIE: "The Impersonation of Saints Among the Pueblos". Papers of the Michigan Academy of Science, Arts and Letters 27: 559-594, 1942.

2. NAVAJO-APACHE

236. HESTER, JAMES J.: Early Navajo Migrations and Acculturation in the Southwest. Santa Fe: MNM Papers in Anthropology No. 6, 1962.

237. HESTER, JAMES J. and JOEL L. SHINER: Studies at Navajo Period Sites in the Navajo Reservoir District. Santa Fe: MNM Papers in Anthropology No. 9, 1964.

238. GUNNERSON, JAMES H. and DOLORES A.: "Evidence of Apaches at Pecos". El Palacio 76/3: 1-6, 1970.
Archeological and documentary evidence of Faraones trade and winter residence at Pecos Pueblo. In the mid-1700's Cuartelejos and Palomas were displaced southward by the Comanches. They had left their women and children at the Pueblo while buffalo hunting. Jicarillas, too, came to Pecos, though more intimate with Taos and Picuris.

239. KIDDER, ALFRED V.: "Ruins of the Historic Period in the Upper San Juan Valley, New Mexico". AA 22/4: 322-329, 1920.
The first article describing residence of Pueblo refugees with Navajos following the 1680 Revolt.

240. MARINO C. C.: "The Seboyetanos and the Navajos". NMHR 29/1: 8-27, 1954.
In the 1850's, prior to settlement of San Mateo, Cebolleta settlers fought with Navajos. They were ambushed at Paraje de San Miguel.

241. MOORHEAD, MAX: The Apache Frontier. Norman: University of Oklahoma Press, 1968.
Apache pressure on southern New Mexico, Arizona and northern Mexico from the late 1760's through the 1780's.

242. REEVE, FRANK D.: "The Navaho-Spanish Wars: 1680-1720". NMHR 33/3: 205-231, 1958.
Aftermath of the Pueblo Revolt.

243. REEVE, FRANK D. "The Navaho-Spanish Peace: 1720-1770's". NMHR 34/1: 9-40, 1959.
Efforts to bring Navajos of the Cebolleta Mountain-Mount Taylor region under missionary control. See Kelly, 1941.

244. REEVE, FRANK D.: "Navaho-Spanish Diplomacy: 1770-1790". NMHR 35/3: 200-235, 1960.
Comanche pressure from the northeast and Apache pressure from the southwest caused Navajos to raid ranches near Cebolleta. Spanish policy to set nomadic tribes against one another caused Navajos and Utes in 1792 to join the Spanish against the Comanches.

245. SCHROEDER, ALBERT H.: "Navajo and Apache Relationships West of the Rio Grande". El Palacio 70/3: 5-23, 1963.
History of intertribal relationships.

246. VAN VALKENBURGH, RICHARD F.: "Tsosi Tells the Story of Massacre Cave". Desert Magazine 3: 22-26, 1940.
In 1805, Sonoran, Opata and New Mexico forces broke Navajo resistance in the Cañon de Chelly.

247. WORCESTER, DONALD E.: "The Beginnings of the Apache Menace in the Southwest". NMHR 16/1: 1-14, 1941.
Between 1630 and 1706 Apaches alternately preyed upon and made alliances with the Pueblos.

248. WORCESTER, DONALD E.: "The Navajo During the Spanish Regime in New Mexico". NMHR 26/2: 101-118, 1951.
Primary sources on Navajo acculturation.

3. UTES AND PLAINS TRIBES

249. BAILEY, L. R.: Indian Slave Trade in the Southwest.
Los Angeles: Westernlore Press, 1966.
See Malouf and Malouf, 1945. Good bibliography.

250. BRUGGE, DAVID M.: "Some Plains Indians in the Church Records of New Mexico". Plains Anthropologist 10/29: 181-189, 1965.
Documentation of Colonial period trade in captives.

251. CHAVEZ, AMADA: "The Defeat of the Comanches in 1717". Albuquerque: Historical Society of New Mexico, Papers, No. 8, 1969.

252. KENNER, CHARLES L.: A History of New Mexican Plains Indian Relations. Norman: University of Oklahoma Press, 1969.
Covers Comanche trade in Colonial-Mexican and Territorial periods but is best for the latter.

253. MALOUF, CARLING and A. ARLINE: "The Effects of Spanish Slavery on the Indians of the Intermountain West". SWJA 1/3: 378-391, 1945.
See Bailey, 1966, for updated study.

254. SCHROEDER, ALBERT H.: "A Brief History of the Southern Utes". Southwestern Lore 30/4: 53-78, 1965.
Southward expansion of Capotes and Moaches in the 1700's and early 1800's, from the northern margins of New Mexico.

255. THOMAS, ALFRED B.: The Plains Indians and New Mexico 1751-1778. Albuquerque: UNM Press, Coronado Cuarto Centennial Publication No. 11, 1940.

256. WALLACE, ERNEST and E. ADAMSON HOEBEL: The Comanches, Lords of the South Plains. Norman: University of Oklahoma Press, 1952.
Good for Comanche lifeways but skimpy on history.

C. HISPANIC NEW MEXICO

257. ADAMS, ELEANOR B., ed.: Bishop Tamaron's Visitation of New Mexico, 1760. Historical Society of New Mexico, Publications in History, No. 15, 1954.
The Episcopal report gives valuable eyewitness information.

258. ADAMS, ELEANOR B." "Viva El Rey!". NMHR 35/4: 284-292, 1960.
Bullfights, dramas and Indian dances celebrated the accession of Ferdinand VI to the throne of Spain in 1760, in far-off New Mexico.

259. ADAMS, ELEANOR B.: "Letter to the Missionaries of New Mexico from Fray Silvestre de Escalante". NMHR 40/4: 319-332, 1965.
This 1777 letter of advice and admonishment reveals much of the hardships and temptations of the isolated missions of New Mexico.

260. ADAMS, ELEANOR B. and FRAY ANGELICO CHAVEZ: The Missions of New Mexico, 1776. Albuquerque: UNM Press, 1956.
The report of Fray Atanacio Dominguez, with other contemporary documents. Well translated and annotated, with 44 fine illustrations.

261. BENAVIDES, FRAY ALONSO DE: The Memorial of Fray Alonso de Benavides, 1630. Mrs. Edward Ayer, trans. Annotated by Frederick Webb Hodge and Charles F. Lummis. Albuquerque: Horn and Wallace, 1965.

262. BENAVIDES, FRAY ALONSO DE: The Revised Memorial of Fray Alonso de Benavides, 1634. Translated and annotated by Frederick W. Hodge, George P. Hammond and Agapito Rey. Albuquerque: UNM Press, 1945.
These are among the earliest and most famous descriptions of New Mexico and her people in early Colonial times.

263. BLOOM, LANSING B.: "New Mexico Under Mexican Administration". Old Santa Fe 1/1: 31-49 (July, 1913); 1/2: 131-175 (October, 1913); 1/3: 235-287 (January, 1914); 1/4: 347-368 (April, 1914); 2/1: 3-56 (July, 1914); 2/2: 119-169 (October, 1914); 2/3: 223-277 (January, 1915); 2/4: 349-380 (April, 1915).
An important compendium on a little-studied period.

264. BOLTON, HERBERT E. trans., annot., etc.: Pageant in the Wilderness: The Diary and Itinerary of Fathers Dominguez and Escalante into the Area Northwest of New Mexico. Salt Lake City: Utah State Historical Society, 1950.

265. BOWDEN, J. J.: Spanish and Mexican Land Grants in the Chihuahuan Acquisition. El Paso: Texas Western Press, 1971.
A sorely needed legal study of grants in southern New Mexico.

266. CARROLL, H. BAILEY and J. VILLASANA HAGGARD: Three New Mexico Chronicles. Albuquerque: The Quivira Society, Vol. 11, 1942.
Pedro Bautista Pino's 1813 report to the Spanish Cortes; Antonio Barreiro's 1832 eyewitness report on New Mexico and Antonio Escudero's recollection of his 1827 visit.

267. CHAVEZ, FRAY ANGELICO: "El Vicatio Don Santiago Roybal". El Palacio 55/8: 231-252, 1948.
The first vicar and ecclesiastical judge of New Mexico (1730-1774).

268. CHAVEZ, FRAY ANGELICO: "Re Gertrudis Barcelo". El Palacio 57/8: 227-234, 1950.
A defense of the owner of a Mexican-period gambling house, who was painted in lurid colors by Josiah Gregg and Susan Magoffin.

269. CHAVEZ, FRAY ANGELICO: "The First Santa Fe Fiesta Council 1712". NMHR 28/3: 183-191, 1953.

270. CHAVEZ, FRAY ANGELICO: Origins of New Mexico Families. Santa Fe: Historical Society of New Mexico, 1954.
Excerpts from Civil and Church Archives relating to the genealogies of present-day Hispanic families of New Mexico. Invaluable. Recently reprinted by the University of Albuquerque.

271. CHAVEZ, FRAY ANGELICO: "The Penitentes of New Mexico". NMHR 29/2: 97-123, 1954.
Valuable material on the maligned and sensationalized lay brotherhood.

272. CHAVEZ, FRAY ANGELICO: "Early Settlements in the Mora Valley". El Palacio 62/11: 318-324, 1955.
300 "souls" were in residence prior to 1818.

273. CHAVEZ, FRAY ANGELICO: "José Gonzales, Genízaro Governor". NMHR 30/3: 190-194, 1955.
Documented material on the 1837 Rebellion; see Reno, 1965.

274. ESPINOSA, GILBERTO and TIBO CHAVEZ: El Río Abajo.
Carter M. Ward, ed. Pampa Print Shop, 1966.
A history of the Belén-Tomé area by two distinguished descendants of early settler families.

275. ESPINOSA, J. MANUEL: Crusaders of the Rio Grande. Chicago: Institute of Jesuit History, 1942.
Documentary data on De Vargas re-entry in 1692 and events to 1700's.

276. FOLMER, HENRI: "Contraband Trade Between Louisiana and New Mexico in the 18th Century". NMHR 16/3: 262-274, 1941.
See also Loomis and Nasater, 1967.

277. GALVEZ, BERNARDO DE. Instructions for Governing the Interior Provinces of New Spain, 1786. Albuquerque: Publications of the Quivira Society, Vol. 12, 1951.
A major Colonial document of exceptional interest. See also Moorhead, 1968.

278. GREENLEAF, RICHARD E.: "The Founding of Albuquerque". NMHR 39/1: 1-15, 1964.
Thirty-five families first settled the "Bosque de Doña Luisa". Doctrine of Pueblo water rights in litigation.

279. HACKETT, CHARLES W., ed. and trans.: Historical Documents Relating to New Mexico, Nueva Vizcaya and Approaches Thereto, to 1773. Washington, D.C.: Carnegie Institute. Vol. 1, 1923; Vol. II, 1926; Vol. III, 1937.
From the splendid documentary collection of Adolph Bandelier.

280. HAMMOND, GEORGE P.: Don Juan de Oñate and the Founding of New Mexico. Albuquerque: Historical Society of New Mexico, Publications in History, No. 2, 1927.
Complete account of Oñate's life and prolonged efforts to bring colonists to New Mexico.

281. HAMMOND, GEORGE P. and AGAPITO REY, eds.: Don Juan de Oñate, Colonizer of New Mexico, 1595-1628. Albuquerque: UNM Press, Coronado Cuarto Gentennial Publications, No. 5-6, 1953.

282. HAMMOND, GEORGE P. and AGAPITO REY: "The Crown's Participation in the Founding of New Mexico". NMHR 32/4: 293-309, 1957.
After the 1601 desertion of one half of Oñate's settlers, Crown authorities assumed full responsibility for holding the New Mexico colony and converting the Indians.

283. KELLY, HENRY W.: *Franciscan Missions of New Mexico 1740-1760.* Albuquerque: Historical Society of New Mexico, Publications in History, No. 10, 1941.
Account of the establishment of a mission for Navajos at Cebolleta, from which the Navajos departed when food ran out. See Reeve, 1959.

284. MILLER, MAMIE T.: *Pueblo Indian Culture as Seen by the Early Spanish Explorers.* Los Angeles: University of Southern California School of Research, Studies, No. 18, Social Science Series, No. 21, 1941.

285. LOOMIS, NOEL M. and ABRAHAM P. NASATER: *Pedro Vial and the Roads to Santa Fe.* Norman: University of Oklahoma Press, 1967.
Trade between New Mexico and Louisiana in the latter 18th century. See Folmer, 1941.

286. MINGE, WARD ALAN: "The Last Will and Testament of Don Severino Martinez". *NM Quarterly 33/1: 33-56, 1963.*
Translation and annotation of a document which provides much information on life in New Mexico in the second quarter of the 19th century.

287. MOORHEAD, MAX L.: *New Mexico's Royal Road: Trade and Travel on the Chihuahua Highway.* Norman: University of Oklahoma Press, 1958.
History of the Camino Real from 1598 to 1848.

288. MOORHEAD, MAX L.: "The Presidio Supply Problem of New Mexico in the Eighteenth Century". *NMHR 36/3: 210-229, 1961.*
Profiteering by Colonial governors and merchants against the pay of the presidial soldiers.

289. PERRIGO, LYNN I.: "New Mexico in the Mexican Period as Revealed in the Torres Documents". *NMHR 29/1: 28-40, 1954.*
Papers of Juan Gerónimo Torres, deceased in Sabinal in 1849. Information on social-economic-legal system of 1822-1846.

290. PUCKETT, FIDELIA M.: "Ramón Ortiz: Priest and Patriot". *NMHR 25/4: 265-295, 1950.*
The life story of a New Mexico leader who, as cura of El Paso, served as commissioner for repatriation in 1846.

291. ROMERO, CECIL V., trans.: "The Apologia of Antonio José Martinez (1838)". *NMHR 3/4: 325-346, 1948.*
This translation reveals the viewpoints of the famous and much-defamed Priest of Taos.

292. SCHOLES, FRANCE V.: "The Supply Service of the New Mexico Missions in the Seventeenth Century". NMHR 5/1: 93-116; 5/2: 186-210; 5/4: 386-404, 1930.
Inventories of supplies are listed.

293. SCHOLES, FRANCE V.: "Civil Government and Society in New Mexico in the Seventeenth Century". NMHR 10/2: 71-111, 1935.
An important study of the composite powers and responsibilities of colonial governors and the status of encomenderos as soldier-citizens.

294. SCHOLES, FRANCE V.: Church and State in New Mexico 1610-1650. Albuquerque: Historical Society of New Mexico, Publications in History, No. 7, 1937.
Conflicts between civil and religious authorities led to abuses against Pueblo Indians, provoking the 1680 Revolt. See Adams and Longhurst, 1953.

295. SIMMONS, MARC: "New Mexico's Smallpox Epidemic of 1780-1781". NMHR 41/4: 319-326, 1966.
Pioneer study of epidemiology of New Mexico.

296. SIMMONS, MARC: Spanish Government in New Mexico. Albuquerque: UNM Press, 1968.
A recent study using many hitherto neglected sources.

297. SIMMONS, MARC: "Spanish Irrigation Practices in New Mexico". NMHR 47/2: 135-150, 1972.
Techniques and vocabulary of irrigation from many primary sources.

298. THOMAS, ALFRED: Forgotten Frontiers: A Study of the Spanish Indian Policy of Juan Bautista de Anza, Governor of New Mexico 1777-1787. Norman: University of Oklahoma Press, 1932.

299. THOMAS, ALFRED B.: Theodoro de Croix and the Northern Frontier of New Spain, 1776-1783. Norman: University of Oklahoma Press, 1941.
Both studies listed above are basic to an understanding of 18th century New Mexico.

300. VILLAGRA, GASPAR PEREZ DE: History of New Mexico. Trans. by Gilberto Espinosa. Los Angeles: Quivira Society, 1933. Reprinted 1962, by Rio Grande Press, Chicago.
An account in verse by one of Oñate's officers in the 1598 entry.

301. WEIGLE, MARTA: The Penitentes of the Southwest. Santa Fe: Ancient City Press, 1970.
Research into published and unpublished sources on the Brotherhood's history.

302. ZARATE SALMERON, FATHER GERONIMO DE: Relaciones. Trans. by Alicia Ronstadt Milich. Albuquerque: Horn and Wallace, 1966.
Eyewitness observations in New Mexico in the 1620's.

D. ANGLO PENETRATION AND CONQUEST

303. ABERT, LT. J. W.: Abert's New Mexico Report 1846-1847. Albuquerque: Horn and Wallace, 1962.
Lt. Abert was a competent observer and lively reporter.

304. ARNOLD, ELLIOT: The Time of the Gringo. New York: Alfred A. Knopf, Inc., 1953.
Historical novel in which Manuel Armijo, Governor of New Mexico just before United States occupation, is the principal character: "villain, conniver, lecher, hero". See Reno, 1965.

305. BLOOM, JOHN P.: "New Mexico Viewed by Anglo-Americans". NMHR 24/3: 165-198, 1958.
Numerous excerpts from soldiers' letters and diaries in the 1840's.

306. CARSON, CHRISTOPHER: Kit Carson's Autobiography. Milo Milton Quaife, ed. Chicago: R. R. Donnelley, 1935.
The Mountain Man who led the campaign against the Navajos.

307. DE VOTO, BERNARD A.: The Year of Decision. Boston: Little Brown and Co, 1943.
Chronological narrative of the United States invasion of Mexico, for the general reader.

308. DICK, EVERETT: Vanguards of the Frontier. Lincoln: University of Nebraska Press, 1941. (Recent paperback reprint).
Social history of Northern Plains-Rocky Mountain-New Mexico Anglo-American settlers.

309. GARRARD, LOUIS: Wah-To-Yah and the Taos Trail. Norman: University of Oklahoma Press, 1962.
First-hand narrative by a young Mountain Man in New Mexico, 1840's.

310. GIBSON, GEORGE R.: Journal of a Soldier Under Kearny and Doniphan 1846-1847. Glendale, California: Arthur H. Clark Co., 1935.
One of the best first-hand accounts of United States forces in New Mexico.

311. GOETZMAN, WILLIAM H.: Army Exploration of the American West (1803-'63). New Haven: Yale University Press, 1969.
Excellent research, covering over half a century of Army records, including New Mexico.

312. GREGG, JOSIAH: Commerce of the Prairies. Norman: University of Oklahoma Press, 1954.
Written 1849. Eyewitness to 1837 Rebellion. Hispanic and Indian life seen through the eyes of a foreigner.

313. HAFEN, LE ROY and ANN W.: Old Spanish Trail: Santa Fe to Los Angeles; With Extracts From Contemporary Records and Including Diaries of Antonio Armijo and Orville Pratt. Glendale, California: Arthur H. Clark Co., 1954.
This route was first reported by Fathers Dominguez and Escalante, who followed it to Central Utah in 1776.

314. HOLMES, KENNETH L.: "The Benjamin Cooper Expeditions to Santa Fe in 1822 and 1823". NMHR 38/2: 139-150, 1963.
Hardships and adventures of early commerce on the Trail.

315. JACKSON, DONALD: The Journals and Papers of Zebulon Montgomery Pike. 2 vols. Norman: University of Oklahoma Press, 1967.
Pike illegally entered New Mexico and was captured and taken to the commandant in Chihuahua in 1807.

316. KENDALL, GEORGE W.: Narrative of the Texas-Santa Fe Expedition. Austin, Texas: Steck, 1936.
1841 expedition, ostensibly for trade, ended in the imprisonment of all participants, including the author, and transportation to Mexico.

317. LOOMIS, NOEL M.: The Texas-Santa Fe Pioneers. Norman: University of Oklahoma Press, 1958.
Efforts of Texas volunteer soldiers in 1841 to extend Texas sovereignty to the Rio Grande. More objective than 316.

318. LOYOLA, SISTER MARY: The American Occupation of New Mexico, 1821-1852. Albuquerque: Historical Society of New Mexico, Publications in History, No. 8, 1939.

319. MAGOFFIN, SUSAN SHELBY: Down the Santa Fe Trail Into Mexico. New Haven: Yale University Press, 1926.
Lively, opinionated narrative by the wife of the United States agent who subverted New Mexican leaders to the American side in 1846.

320. MERK, FREDERICK: Manifest Destiny and Mission in American History. New York: Random House (A Vintage Book), 1966.
Study of United States public opinion concerning expansionism, starting with the Mexican War.

321. PARKHILL, FORBES: The Blazed Trail of Antoine Leroux. Los Angeles: Westernlore Press, 1965.
Story of a Canadian Mountain Man in New Mexico.

322. PORTER, CLYDE and MAE REED: Ruxton of the Rockies. Norman; University of Oklahoma Press, 1950.
Ruxton's 1846-8 trip from Veracruz to Mexico City and northward to New Mexico and Colorado. The young Britisher died in St. Louis in 1848.

323. RENO, PHILIP: "Rebellion in New Mexico, 1837". NMHR 40/3: 197-213, 1965.
Documents the United States role in the Rebellion and Armijo's two-faced connivance. See Arnold, 1953.

324. RUSSELL, CARL P.: Firearms, Traps and Tools of the Mountain Men. New York: Alfred A. Knopf, Inc., 1967.

325. SMITH, RALPH A.: "Apache Plunder Trails Southward 1831-1840". NMHR 40/3: 215-232, 1962.
The "scalp captain", James Kirker, for a price, collected Apache scalps for the comandante of Chihuahua -- or sometimes joined the Apaches to scalp Mexicans.

326. VESTAL, STANLEY: The Old Santa Fe Trail. New York: Houghton Mifflin (Bantam), 1939.
A popular work.

327. WEBER, DAVID J.: Taos Trappers: The Fur Trade in the Far Southwest. Norman: University of Oklahoma Press, 1971.
Based on untapped primary sources in Mexico.

328. YOUNG, OTIS E.: The First Military Escort on the Santa Fe Trail 1829: From the Journal and Reports of Major Bennet Riley and Lieutenant Philip St. George Cooke. Glendale, California: Arthur H. Clark Co., 1952.
"...gives a clear picture of the organization of a caravan. It shows the trials and dangers on the trail; and the life of the troops on the march and in camp".

IV. TERRITORIAL PERIOD

A. PUEBLOS: TRESPASS

329. BINNER, WITTER: "From Him That Hath Not". Outlook 133: 125-127, 1923.
Protest against a bill to legalize claims of non-Indian squatters on Indian lands.

330. BRAYER, HERBERT O.: Pueblo Indian Grants of the Rio Abajo, New Mexico. Albuquerque: UNM Press, 1939.

331. CLARK, ROBERT E.: "The Pueblo Rights Doctrine in New Mexico". NMHR 35/4: 265-283, 1960.
Discussion of Pueblo water rights issue.

332. COLLIER, JOHN: "The Pueblo Lands". Survey 65: 548-549, 1936.
Anglo encroachments on Indian lands and resulting legal tangles.

B. NAVAJO-APACHE: WARS

333. ARNOLD, ELLIOT: Blood Brother. New York: Duell, Sloan and Pierce, 1947.
Canby's campaign against the Gila River Apaches in the 1860's was far from a success.

334. BOURKE, JOHN G.: On the Border With Crook. Glorieta: The Rio Grande Press, Inc., 1969.
Originally published in 1892, the narrative of the 1869 Apache and Navajo campaigns, sandwiched among Northern Plains campaigns.

335. CREMONY, JOHN C.: Life Among the Apaches. Glorieta: The Rio Grande Press, Inc., 1969.
First published 1868, an eyewitness account of the Apache campaigns of the 1860's.

336. FRAZER, ROBERT W., ed.: New Mexico in 1850: A Military View. Norman: University of Oklahoma Press, 1968.
Col. McCall's military report of combat and preparations for combat, with a good introduction by the editor.

337. GARDNER, HAMILTON: "Philip St. George Cooke and the Apache, 1854". NMHR 28/2: 115-132, 1953.
A campaign against the Jicarillas, from Ojo Caliente into the San Luis Valley. See Taylor, 1969.

338. KELEHER, WILLIAM A.: Turmoil in New Mexico. Santa Fe: Rydal Press, 1952.
A very readable account, from the late 1840's through the Navajo captivity at the Bosque Redondo and the Civil War.

339. KELLY, LAWRENCE: Navajo Roundup: Selected Correspondence of Kit Carson's Expedition Against the Navajo, 1863-1865. Boulder: Pruett Press, 1970.
A new view of the last Navajo campaign and of Carson's role.

340. LAMAR, HOWARD R.: The Far Southwest, 1846-1912: A Territorial History. New York: W. W. Norton and Co., Inc., 1970.
Most thorough coverage, from primary documentary sources. Deals with New Mexico from about 1810, also covers those portions of Arizona, Utah and Colorado, formerly a part of New Mexico.

341. LINDGREN, RAYMOND E.: "A Diary of Kit Carson's Navajo Campaign 1863-1864". NMHR 21/3: 226-247, 1946.
See Kelly, 1970 for more recent, complete coverage.

342. RICKEY, DON, JR.: Forty Miles a Day on Beans and Hay: The Enlisted Soldier Fighting the Indian Wars. Norman: University of Oklahoma Press, 1963.
Mostly pertaining to Northern Plains but applicable to Southwest.

343. SONNICHSEN, C. L.: The Mescalero Apaches. Norman: University of Oklahoma Press, 1958. Historical struggles of Mescaleros over two centuries. Critical evaluation of General Carleton's Apache policy. Ends with 1880.

344. TAYLOR, MORRIS F.: "Campaigns Against the Jicarilla Apache 1854". NMHR 44/4: 269-291, 1969.
See Gardner, 1958.

345. UTLEY, ROBERT M.: Frontiersmen in Blue: The United States Army and the Indian 1848-1865. New York: The Macmillan Company, 1967.
Focus on the Southwest, explanation of campaign strategy.

346. WILSON, JOHN P.: Military Campaigns in the Navajo Country. Santa Fe: MNM Research Records, No. 5, 1967.
Thorough summary.

C. HISPANOS: LAND LOSS

347. ATENCIO, THOMAS C.: "The Human Dimensions of Land Use and Land Displacement in Northern New Mexico Villages", in Indian and Spanish Adjustments to Arid and Semiarid Environments, Clark S. Knowlton, ed. Lubbock: Texas Technological College, 1964.
A study relating culture to land use and land loss.

348. BLACKMAR, FRANK W.: Spanish Institutions of the Southwest. Baltimore: Johns Hopkins, 1891.
Old but good study of legal system and its eclipse. Focus on land.

349. BRAYER, HERBERT O.: William Blackmore: The Spanish-Mexican Land Grants of New Mexico and Colorado, 1863-1878. 2 vols. Denver: Bradford-Robinson, 1949.
Detailed study of one of the European land-grant speculators.

350. CHANDLER, ALFRED N.: Land Title Origins: Force and Fraud. Schalkenback Foundation, 1945.

351. DUNHAM, HAROLD H.: "New Mexican Land Grants With Special Reference to the Title Papers of the Maxwell Land Grant". NMHR 30/1: 1-22, 1955.
Describes fraudulent methods used to gain and transfer titles.

352. GILBERT, FABIOLA C. DE BACA: We Fed Them Cactus. Albuquerque: UNM Press, 1954.
Life on a cattle and sheep ranch on the Staked Plain during the Territorial Period.

353. GOODRICH, JAMES W.: "Revolt at Mora, 1847". NMHR 47/1: 49-60, 1972.
Delayed-reaction efforts to shake off Anglo-American domination. It was, however, too late.

354. KELEHER, WILLIAM A.: "Law of the New Mexico Land Grant". NMHR 4/4: 350-371, 1929.
A lawyer's view of the grants and problems of obtaining merchantable title.

355. McCARTY, FRANKIE: Land Grant Problems in New Mexico. Albuquerque: Albuquerque Journal (pamphlet), 1969.
Readable and interesting.

356. OTERO, MIGUEL A.: My Nine Years as Governor of the Territory of New Mexico 1897-1906. Albuquerque: UNM Press, 1940.

357. PEARSON, JIM B.: The Maxwell Land Grant. Norman: University of Oklahoma Press, 1961.
History of the Grant and of the Maxwell Mining Company, with its British promoters, Dutch mortgage holders and absentee owners, etc.

358. TAYLOR, MARGUERITE W.: "The Crumbling Walls of Chamberino". NMHR 39/3: 169-180, 1964.
History of the Refugio Colony from the time of its settlement by refugees from U.S. domination in 1848 through its reincorporation into New Mexico by terms of the Gadsden Purchase, and into the twentieth century.

359. TAYLOR, MORRIS F.: Treaty of Guadalupe Hidalgo. Truchas: The Tate Gallery, 1967. (Reprint).

360. TAYLOR, MORRIS F.: "Bent Heirs' Claim to the Maxwell Land Grant". NMHR 43/3: 213-228, 1968.
Reviews years of complex litigation, as the boundaries claimed for the Grant expanded to include nearly two million acres.

361. WALTER, PAUL A. F.: Colonel José Francisco Chavez 1833-1924. Albuquerque: Historical Society of New Mexico, Papers, No. 131, 1926.
A prominent New Mexican whose life spanned three governments.

362. WESTPHALL, VICTOR: The Public Domain in New Mexico 1854-1891. Albuquerque: UNM Press, 1965.
Well-documented study with numerous maps, tables and appendices.

D. ANGLOS

1. CIVIL WAR

363. FOSTER, JAMES M., JR.: "Fort Bascom, New Mexico". NMHR 35/1: 30-62, 1960.
Civil War fort on the Canadian River near present-day Tucumcari, used to curb Kiowas and Comanches, later to control Navajos at the Bosque Redondo.

364. HALL, MARTIN H.: Sibley's New Mexico Campaign. Austin: University of Texas Press, 1960.
Confederate invasion of New Mexico in 1862, under Texas banner.

365. HORN AND WALLACE, eds.: Confederate Victories in the Southwest: Prelude to Defeat. Albuquerque: Horn and Wallace, 1961.
Transcripts of Civil War documents covering events in New Mexico up to the capture of Santa Fe.

366. HORN AND WALLACE, eds.: Union Army Operations in the Southwest: Final Victory. Albuquerque: Horn and Wallace, 1961.
More transcripts of Civil War documents.

367. LECKIE, WILLIAM H.: The Buffalo Soldiers: A Narrative of The Negro Cavalry in the West. Norman: University of Oklahoma Press, 1967.
Many Black soldiers settled in New Mexico after the Civil War.

368. NOEL, THEO: A Campaign From Santa Fe to the Mississippi: Being a History of the Old Sibley Brigade. Houston: Stagecoach Press, 1961.
Eyewitness description, written in 1865, of the Texan invasion of New Mexico. This edition includes footnotes and a concise, objective introduction.

2. FRONTIER VIOLENCE

369. FULTON, MAURICE G.: History of the Lincoln County War. Robert N. Mullin, ed. Tucson: University of Arizona Press. (Reprint), 1968.
The definitive work on Lincoln County, written in the 1920's after interviews with survivors.

370. HINTON, HARWOOD P., JR.: "John Simpson Chisum 1877-84". NMHR 31/3: 177-205; 31-4: 310-337, 1956; 32/1: 53-65, 1957.
Focus on the late 1870's, with early history of Roswell.

371. KELEHER, WILLIAM A.: Violence in Lincoln County. Albuquerque: UNM Press, 1957.
Highly readable account with some inaccuracies.

372. NOLAN, FREDERICK W.: The Life and Death of John Henry Tunstall: The Letters, Diaries and Adventures of an Itinerant Englishman. Albuquerque: UNM Press, 1965.
Tunstall was a victim of Lincoln County violence.

373. POTTER, CHESTER D.: "Reminiscences of the Socorro Vigilantes", Paige W. Christiansen, ed. NMHR 40/1: 23-54, 1965.
Describes a lynching bee by the Socorro "Committee of Safety" in the 1880's and the involvement of wealthy land grant manipulator Colonel Eaton.

374. RASCH, PHILIP: "The Horrell War". NMHR 31/3: 223-281, 1956.
Events in Lincoln County in 1874 reflected chronic hostility between Hispano residents and Texas cowboys supposedly grubstaked by L. G. Murphy and Co.

375. RASCH, PHILIP: "Exit Axtell: Enter Wallace". NMHR 32/3: 231-245, 1957.
Close-up of Lincoln County situation in 1878, resulting from Governor Wallace's failure to assess the situation correctly.

376. RASCH, PHILIP: "The Rustler War". NMHR 39/4: 257-273, 1964.
Banditti led by John Kinney of Rincón in early 1880's committed large-scale theft, and militia was called out.

377. RASCH, PHILIP: "Feuding at Farmington". NMHR 40/3: 215-232, 1965.
Vigilantism and lawlessness from San Juan Basin to Tierra Amarilla and involvement of Adjutant General, Max Frost, in counter-measures.

3. RANCHING, BUSINESS AND TRANSPORTATION

378. CLEAVELAND, AGNES MORLEY: No Life for a Lady. Boston: Houghton Mifflin Co., 1941.
Early ranching life in the Magdalena Mountains, wittily told.

379. COOLIDGE, DANE: <u>Lorenzo the Magnificent</u>. New York: Dutton, 1925.
Life of Lorenzo Hubbell, Navajo trader of Ganado. See Section VI.

380. FRENCH, WILLIAM: <u>Some Recollections of a Western Ranchman in New Mexico, 1883-1889</u>. London: Methuen, 1927.

381. GREEVER, WILLIAM S.: "Railway Development in the Southwest". <u>NMHR 32/2: 151-203, 1957</u>.
In the 1870's and 1880's tycoons competed for control of routes.

382. GRUBBS, FRANK H.: "Frank Bond: Gentleman Sheepherder of Northern New Mexico". <u>NMHR 36/2: 138-158; 36/3: 230-243; 36/4: 274-345, 1961; 37/1: 43-71, 1962</u>.
Record of the rise of large livestock and banking interests in northern New Mexico in the latter 19th century.

383. KELEHER, WILLIAM A.: <u>The Fabulous Frontier: Twelve New Mexico Items</u>. Albuquerque: <u>UNM Press (Revised edition), 1962</u>.
Biographies of twelve Lincoln County men of Territorial times.

384. McCOY, JOSEPH G.: <u>Historic Sketches of the Cattle Trade of the West and Southwest</u>. Ralph P. Bieber, ed. Glendale, California: Arthur H. Clark Co., 1940. Southwest Historical Series, No. 8.

385. McNITT, FRANK: <u>The Indian Traders</u>. Norman: University of Oklahoma Press, 1962.
Archival and journalistic sources on the Navajo trade of northwestern New Mexico and northeastern Arizona in Post-Civil War period.

386. PARISH, WILLIAM J.: "The German Jew and the Commercial Revolution in Territorial New Mexico, 1850-1900". <u>NMHR 35/1: 1-29; 35/2: 129-150, 1960</u>.
Jewish merchants catalyzed relatively peaceful convergence of people of different cultures around a new set of commercial relations.

387. PARISH, WILLIAM J.: <u>The Charles Ilfeld Company</u>. Cambridge: Harvard University Press, 1961.
A large business enterprise from Territorial times to 1930's.

388. PARISH, WILLIAM J.: "Sheep Husbandry in New Mexico 1902-1903". NMHR 37/3: 201-213; 37/4: 260-309, 1961; 38/1: 56-77, 1962. See also Grubbs 1961-1962.

389. ROBB, JOHN D.: "Sheep Shearing in New Mexico, 1956". NMHR 32/4: 357-360, 1957.
Description of procedures which have not changed since mechanical clippers were introduced 1895-1905.

390. SCHAEFER, JACK: Heroes Without Glory: Some Goodmen of the Old West. New York: Houghton Mifflin Co., 1965.
Short biographies of ten men including George Ruxton and Elfego Baca.

391. STEWART, F.J.: Penny-an-acre Empire in the West. Norman: University of Oklahoma Press, 1968.
Includes rare documents on Fort Sumner and many land matters.

392. WADLEIGH, A. B.: "Ranching in New Mexico, 1886-90". NMHR 26/2: 1-28, 1952.
Open-range cattle ranching in various parts of New Mexico. Reflects individualism and anti-Mexican bias of Anglo cattlemen and miners.

393. WALLACE, WILLIAM S.: "Short-Line Staging in New Mexico". NMHR 26/2: 89-100, 1951.
The Lake-Valley-Hillsboro and Kingston Line ran until 1904.

394. WALLACE, WILLIAM S.: "Stagecoaching in Territorial New Mexico". NMHR 32/2: 204-210, 1957.
Stagecoaching began in 1840's; after 1879 feeder lines ran to railroad termini.

4. ADMINISTRATION AND THE STATEHOOD QUESTION

395. BOYD, NATHAN E.: New Mexico and Statehood. Washington: Judd and Detweiler, 1902.
A contemporaneous study while statehood was at issue.

396. HORN, CALVIN: New Mexico's Troubled Years, the Story of the Early Territorial Governors. Albuquerque: Horn and Wallace, 1963.
The best work available on this period.

397. HUNT, AURORA: <u>Kirby Benedict: Frontier Federal Judge</u>. Glendale, California: Arthur H. Clark Co., 1961.
From Benedict papers and official documents, depiction of the Civil War-time Chief Justice of the Territorial Supreme Court, who was at other times a newspaper editor.

398. LAMAR, HOWARD R.: "Edward G. Ross as Governor of New Mexico Territory: a Reappraisal". <u>NMHR 36/3: 179-209, 1961</u>.
Territorial politics 1885-1889 under a reform governor.

399. LARSON, ROBERT W.: <u>New Mexico's Quest for Statehood</u>. Albuquerque: UNM Press, 1968.
Supersedes other works on the statehood issue.

400. LEOPARD, DONALD D.: "Joint Statehood: 1906". <u>NMHR 34/4: 241-247, 1959</u>.
New Mexico nearly became part of a state jointly with Arizona.

401. POLDEVAART, ARIE W.: <u>Black-Robed Justice: A History of the Administration of Justice in New Mexico from the American Occupation in 1846 Until Statehood in 1912</u>. Albuquerque: UNM Press, 1948.

402. TWITCHELL, RALPH EMERSON: <u>The History of the Military Occupation of New Mexico From 1846 to 1851...together with biographical sketches of men in the conduct of the government during that period</u>. Denver: Smith-Brooks Co., 1909.
Recently reprinted by Rio Grande Press, Glorieta, New Mexico.

V. <u>RECENT HISTORY: CHANGE IN CULTURE AND INSTITUTIONS</u>

A. <u>GENERAL</u>

403. ADAIR, JOHN and EVON Z. VOGT: "Navajo and Zuni Veterans: A Study of Contrasting Modes of Culture Change". <u>AA 51/4: 547-561, 1949</u>.
Changes brought about by Army service and the reactions of the home society.

404. BUNKER, ROBERT: Other Men's Skies. Bloomington: University of Indiana Press, 1956.
Discussion of Bureau of Indian Affairs policy versus Indian objectives by a former BIA official of the Pueblo Agency.

405. CAHN, EDGAR S. (ed.): Our Brother's Keeper: The Indian in White America. Cleveland: World Publishing Book Co. A New Community Press Book, 1969.
Chapter and verse on government bureaucracy and cultural genocide suffered by Indians.

406. COLLIER, JOHN: "New Policies in Indian Education". NM Quarterly 3: 202-206, 1933.
Statement of the philosophy behind New Deal Indian education policy.

407. FERGUSSON, ERNA: "From Redskins to Railroads". Century Magazine 113:23-31, 1926.
Changes in New Mexico life from the early Territorial period.

408. HAWLEY, FLORENCE and DONOVAN SENTER: "Group Designed Behavior in Two Acculturating Groups". SWJA 2/2: 133-151, 1946.
Contrasts changes among Pueblo Indians with those of Hispanos.

409. KLUCKHOHN, CLYDE: "Hopi and Navaho". NM Quarterly 3: 56-64, 1933.
Contrasting characteristics of the two groups.

410. MAES, ERNEST: "The Labor Movement in New Mexico". NM Business Review 4/2: 137-140, 1935.

411. MEADERS, MARGARET: "Copper Chronicle: The Story of New Mexico's 'Red Gold'". New Mexico Business 11/5: 2-9, 11/6: 2-9, 1958.
Industrial growth in New Mexico has been largely based on the extractive industries.

412. MUNCH, FRANCIS J.: "Villa's Columbus Raid". NMHR 44/3: 189-214, 1969.
Circumstances surrounding the raid, plus contemporary photos.

413. SMITH, ANNE M.: New Mexico Indians: Economic, Educational and Social Problems. Santa Fe: MNM Research Records No. 1, 1966.
The most up-to-date compendium on all tribes, with valuable analysis. Quantitative data are largely based on 1960 Census.

414. SMITH, ANNE M.: Indian Education in New Mexico.
Albuquerque: UNM Division of Government Research, Institute for
Social Research and Development, No. 77, 1968.
Focus on current educational problems.

415. SMITH, ANNE M.: "Indian Head Start". El Palacio 75/4:
12-30, 1968.
Bureaucracy versus innovation in a pre-school program.

416. SPICER, EDWARD H.: "Spanish-Indian Acculturation in the
Southwest". AA 56/3: 663-684, 1954.
Deals with five types of contact adjustment during the Spanish
Colonial period.

417. SPICER, EDWARD H.: Cycles of Conquest. Tucson: University
of Arizona Press, 1962.
Has good coverage of Pueblo and Navajo changes.

418. ZERWEKH, SISTER EDWARD MARY, CSJ: "Jean Baptiste
Salpointe, 1825-1894". NMHR 37/1: 1-19; 37/2: 132-154;
37/3: 214-229, 1962.
History of the Catholic Church in New Mexico in transition under
United States Territorial rule.

B. PUEBLOS

419. ANDERSON, FRANK GIBBS: "The Pueblo Indian Kachina Cult:
A Historical Reconstruction". SWJA 11/4: 404-419, 1955.

420. APPLEGATE, FRANK: "Sandia the Tragic". Southwest Review
15/3: 310-316, 1932.
History of Sandia since the Spanish Conquest.

421. DOZIER, EDWARD P.: "The Rio Grande Pueblos", in
Perspectives in American Indian Culture Change: 94-186,
Edward H. Spicer, ed. Chicago: University of Chicago Press, 1961.
Detailed, excellently documented study in historic depth.

422. ELLIS, FLORENCE HAWLEY: "An Outline of Laguna Pueblo
History and Social Organization". SWJA 15/4: 325-347, 1959.

423. ELLIS, FLORENCE HAWLEY: <u>A Reconstruction of the Basic Jemez Pattern of Social Organization, with Comparisons to Other Tanoan Social Structures</u>. Albuquerque: UNM Publications in Anthropology, No. 11, 1964.
Synthesis.

424. FENTON, WILLIAM N.: "Factionalism at Taos Pueblo". <u>BAE Bull. No. 164: 297-346, 1957</u>.
Factionalism is both a catalyst and a consequence of change.

425. FEWKES, J. WALTER: "The Pueblo Settlements Near El Paso". <u>AA 4/1: 57-72, 1902</u>.
Post-1680 Tiwa settlement of Ysleta, Texas and Piros settlements of San Antonio Senecú, Chihuahua and Socorro, Texas. Present Mexicanized "Indian" dances are survivals of ritual without context of beliefs. Tiwa is still spoken by some at Ysleta. Caciques' duties are codified.

426. FOX, ROBIN: <u>The Keresan Bridge</u>. London School of Economics: Monographs in Social Anthropology, No. 35, 1967.
The data are mainly from Cochiti, but the problems of the position of the Keresans in general are examined.

427. FRENCH, DAVID H.: <u>Factionalsim in Isleta Pueblo</u>. New York: American Ethnological Society, Monograph No. 14, 1948.
Compare with Fenton, 1957.

428. HALSETH, ODD S.: "Report on the Economic and Social Survey of the Keres Pueblo of Zia, New Mexico". <u>El Palacio 16/5: 67-75, 1924</u>.
General account of conditions at Zia to 1923.

429. HAWLEY, FLORENCE: "Pueblo Social Organization as a Lead to Pueblo History." <u>AA 39/3: 504-522, 1937</u>.
Hawley concludes that Hopi and Zuñi influences account for Acoma and Jemez exogamous matrilineal clans, as well as Hano. Tewa have dual organization and Tiwa are divergent.

430. HAWLEY, FLORENCE: <u>Some Factors in the Indian Problems in New Mexico</u>. Albuquerque: UNM Division of Research, Department of Government, 1948.

431. HURT, WESLEY R., JR.: "Notes on the Santa Ana Indians". <u>El Palacio 48/6: 131-142, 1941</u>.
Contact and change in the village of El Ranchito to which the Santa Ana population has moved.

432. HURT, WESLEY R., JR.: "Tortugas, An Indian Village in Southern New Mexico". El Palacio 59/4: 104-122, 1952.
Remnant Tiwa-Manso and "Mexican Indian" groups near Las Cruces.

433. LANGE, CHARLES H.: "The Role of Economics in Cochiti Pueblo Culture Change". AA 55/5: 674-694, 1953.

434. LANGE, CHARLES H.: "A Reappraisal of Plains Influence Among the Rio Grande Pueblos". SWJA 9/1: 212-230, 1953.
Hypothesis of Pueblo adaptation to Plains traits "adjusted to conform to existing Pueblo patterns". Technical, but interesting.

435. LANGE, CHARLES H.: Cochiti: A New Mexico Pueblo, Past and Present. Austin : University of Texas Press, 1959.
A very inclusive study: history, ethnography, current changes using all previous Cochiti studies.

436. O'BRYAN, DERIC: "The Abandonment of the Northern Pueblos in the Thirteenth Century", in The Indian Tribes of Aboriginal America, Sol Tax, ed. Chicago: University of Chicago Press, 1952.
Puebloan regional migrations in prehispanic times, as an explanation of change.

437. PARSONS, ELSIE CLEWS: "The Laguna Migration to Isleta". AA 30/4: 602-613, 1928.
A conservative reaction to change within the Pueblo.

438. SEKAQUAPTEWA, HELEN (as Told to Louise Udall): Me and Mine. Tucson: University of Arizona Press, 1969.
The autobiography of a Hopi woman who sought the best of both the Hopi and Anglo-American worlds.

439. SIEGEL, BERNARD J.: "Some Observations on the Pueblo Pattern at Taos". AA 51/4: 562-577, 1949.
Conflict between ideal (collectivistic) and actual (individualistic) patterns during a period of intense change.

440. SIMONS, SUZANNE L.: "The Cultural and Social Survival of a Pueblo Indian Community", in Minorities and Politics: 85-112, Henry J. Tobias and Charles E. Woodhouse, eds., Albuquerque: UNM Press, 1969.
Change and stability in Sandia Pueblo.

441. SPIER, LESLIE L.: "The Pueblos Since Coronado". El Palacio 47/9: 201-204, 1940.
Concise summary of Pueblo life as Coronado witnessed it and as it was in 1940.

442. WHITMAN, WILLIAM: "The San Ildefonso of New Mexico", in Acculturation in Seven American Indian Tribes: 390-462, Ralph Linton, ed. New York and London: D. Appleton-Century Co., 1940.
Important because of the scarcity of material on this Tewa Pueblo.

C. NAVAJO-APACHE

443. ABERLE, DAVID F.: The Peyote Religion Among the Navajo. New York: Viking Fund Publications in Anthropology, No. 42, 1966.
A well-documented study of factors involved in change.

444. BENNETT, KAY: Kaibah: Recollections of a Navajo Girlhood. Los Angeles: Westernlore Press, 1964.
The autobiography of a New Mexico Navajo girl during the years 1928-1935.

445. CARLSON, VADA and GARY WITHERSPOON: Black Mountain Boy: A Story of the Boyhhod of John Honie. Rough Rock, Arizona: Navajo Curriculum Center, 1968.
The biography of a contemporary medicine man, born and raised in the early 20th century, designed to enhance the self-image of the Navajo schoolchild. The Rough Rock Demonstration School is using books in English and Navajo prepared by the Curriculum Center. Fine illustrations by Andy Tsinajinnie.

446. HILL, W. W.: "Stability in Culture and Pattern". AA 41/2: 258-260, 1939.
Variations in the Navajo Night Chant, with evidence of resistance even to those changes which were in harmony with the existing logic of imitative and contagious magic. See 698.

447. HILL, W. W.: "Some Navaho Culture Changes During Two Centuries". Smithsonian Misc. Coll., Vol. 100: 395-415, 1940.
Includes a translation of the early 18th century Rabal Ms.

448. KIMBALL, SOLON T. and JOHN H. PROVINSE: "Navajo Social Organization in Land Use Planning". Applied Anthropology 1/1: 18-30, 1942.
A social structural study in the context of community development.

449. KLUCKHOHN, CLYDE: "The Navajos in the Machine Age". The Technology Review 44/1: 2-6, 1942.
A study of contact-induced culture change.

450. MITCHELL, EMERSON BLACKHORSE: Miracle Hill: The Story of a Navajo Boy. Norman: University of Oklahoma Press, 1967.
Autobiographical account of a young Navajo's life, relationships with his own family and dealing with the world of the white man.

451. MR. MOUSTACHE: "A Navajo Personal Document", Clyde Kluckhohn, ed., SWJA 1/2: 260-283, 1945.
A brief autobiography, describes social conditioning in Navajo value system.

452. OLD MEXICAN: A Navajo Autobiography, as told to Walter Dyk. New York: Viking Fund Publications in Anthropology, No. 8, 1947.
Narrative runs from 1871, when the narrator was five years old, to 1919, and deals mainly with adult life in Navajo society.

453. SASAKI, TOM: Fruitland, New Mexico: A Navajo Community in Transition. Ithaca, New York: Cornell University Press, 1960.
Report on an attempt at planned change and its pitfalls.

454. SASAKI, TOM and HARRY W. BASEHART: "Changing Political Organization in the Jicarilla Apache". Human Organization 23/4: 283-289, 1964.
An excellent study of transition, one of the few about Jicarillas.

455. SHEPARDSON, MARY and BLODWEN HAMMOND: The Navajo Mountain Community. Berkeley: University of California, 1970.
Well-organized results of field research on Navajo Mountain.

456. SON OF FORMER MANY BEADS: The Ramah Navajos, Robert W. Young and William Morgan, eds. Lawrence, Kansas: Haskell Institute Publications Service, 1967.
Bilingual borchure, dealing with matters of historical import to the Navajos and with land problems of Ramah, New Mexico area.

457. STEINER, STAN: The New Indians. New York: Harper and Row, 1968.
Description of the Red Power movement and some of its leaders.

458. UNDERHILL, RUTH: Here Come the Navajo. Haskell, Kansas: U.S. Indian Service, 1953.
Prepared for BIA schoolchildren, an outstandingly good treatment of Navajo culture and culture change.

459. VOGT, EVON Z.: "Navaho" in Perspectives in American Indian Culture Change, Edward Spicer, ed.: 278-336. Chicago: University of Chicago Press, 1961.
Detailed, excellently documented study in historic depth.

460. WORTH, SOL and JOHN ADAIR: "Navajo Filmmakers". AA 70/1: 9-34, 1970.
The results of an experiment in filmmaking in which Navajos recorded in their own way their view of the world.

D. HISPANO

461. BLAWIS, PATRICIA BELL: Tijerina and The Land Grants. New York: International Publishers Company, Inc., 1971.
Very readable, well-documented eyewitness account of the New Mexico land-grant movement in the context of current struggles of oppressed people.

462. EDMONSON, MONRO: Los Manitos: A Study of Institutional Values. New Orleans: Tulane University, Middle American Research Institute, Publ. No. 25, 1957.
Data from several late settlements in the Gallup-Ramah area, divergent from older Hispanic communities in northern New Mexico.

463. GONZALEZ, NANCIE L.: The Spanish Americans of New Mexico. Albuquerque: UNM Press, 1969.
Recently compiled from the works of many previous authors.

464. HENDERSON, ALICE CORBIN: Brothers of Light: The Penitentes of the Southwest. New York: Harcourt, Brace and Company, 1937. Reprinted 1962 by Rio Grande Press.
Describes Holy Week in Abiquiu.

465. JARAMILLO, CLEOFAS M.: Shadows of the Past. Santa Fe: Seton Village Press, 1941. (Reprinted, Santa Fe: Ancient City Press, 1972).
Authentic, first-hand account of village life.

466. JARAMILLO, CLEOFAS M.: Romance of a Little Village Girl.
San Antonio, Texas: Naylor Co., 1955.
Autobiographical, readable from age 12 through adult years.

467. KLUCKHOHN, FLORENCE R.: "The Spanish Americans of Atrisco" in Variations in Value Orientations: 175-257, Florence Kluckhohn and Fred Strodtbeck, eds. Evanston, Illinois and Elmsford, New York: Row, Peterson and Co., 1961.
"Atrisco" is a pseudonym. See 489.

468. KNOWLTON, CLARK S.: "One Approach to the Economic and Social Problems of New Mexico". New Mexico Business 17/9: 3, 15-22, 1964.
Relates the socio-economic decline of Hispanos to land loss and social subordination.

469. LEONARD, OLEN: The Role of the Land Grant in the Social Organization and Social Processes of a Spanish-American Village in New Mexico. Ann Arbor: Edwards Press, 1943.
Historical study of El Cerrito, a community in the Pecos Valley. Recently reprinted by Horn and Wallace.

470. LEONARD, OLEN and CHARLES P. LOOMIS: Culture of a Contemporary Rural Community: El Cerrito, New Mexico. Washington, D.C.: U.S. Bureau of Agricultural Economics, Rural Life Studies, 1941.
Another study of El Cerrito.

471. LOOMIS, CHARLES P.: "Informal Groupings in a Spanish-American Village". Sociometry 41/1: 36-51, 1941.
Study of the extended kin group in El Cerrito, New Mexico.

472. LOOMIS, CHARLES P.: "Wartime Migrations from Rural Spanish-Speaking Villages of New Mexico". Rural Sociology 7/4: 384-395, 1942.
Record of a period of sweeping change in El Cerrito.

473. LOOMIS, CHARLES P.: "Ethnic Cleavages in the Southwest as Reflected in Two High Schools". Sociometry 6/1: 7-26, 1943.
Anglo and Hispano in the high schools attended by El Cerrito youth.

474. LOOMIS, CHARLES P.: "El Cerrito, New Mexico: A Changing Village". NMHR 33/1: 53-75, 1958.
Postwar impoverishment and depopulation.

475. LOOMIS, CHARLES P. and GLEN GRISHAM: "Spanish Americans: The New Mexico Experiment in Village Rehabilitation". Applied Anthropology 2/3: 13-37, 1943.
Record of a Pecos Valley livestock cooperative and introduction of modern farming methods in the late Thirties.

476. MAES, ERNEST E.: "The World and People of Cundiyo". Land Policy Review 4: 8-14, 1941.
Porblems of Cundiyo as typical of the Hispanic villages of northern New Mexico.

477. MALONEY, THOMAS J.: "Recent Demographic and Economic Changes in Northern New Mexico". New Mexico Business 17/9: 2, 4-14, 1964.
A study of rural depopulation in the years following World War Two.

478. OBERG, KALERVO: "Cultural Factors and Land-Use Planning in Cuba Valley, New Mexico". Rural Sociology 5/4: 438-448, 1940.

479. RENDON, GABINO: Hand on My Shoulder. New York: Board of National Missions, The United Presbyterian Church in the U.S.A., 1955.
Autobiography of a catalytic leader, one of the first Hispano Presbyterian ministers.

480. SAMORA, JULIAN, ed.: La Raza: Forgotten Americans. Notre Dame: University of Notre Dame Press, 1966.
The chapter on New Mexico contains statistical analysis, based on the U.S. Census of 1960. Other chapters treat problems relevant to New Mexico's situation.

481. SANCHEZ, George I.: Forgotten People: A Study of New Mexicans. Albuquerque: UNM Press, 1940. (Reprinted Albuquerque: Horn and Wallace Press, 1967).
Although focussed on socioeconomic problems of Taos County in the Depression years, the problems depicted are widespread and still current.

482. SANCHEZ, GEORGE I.: "New Mexico and Acculturation". NMQR 11/1: 61-68, 1941.
Analysis of the causes of educational "backwardness" of Hispanic New Mexicans.

483. SENTER, DONOVAN: "Acculturation Among New Mexican Villagers in Comparison to Adjustment Patterns of Other Spanish-Speaking Americans". Rural Sociology 10/1: 31-47, 1945.

484. STEINER, STAN: La Raza: The Mexican-Americans. New York: Harper and Row, 1969.
Journalistic vignettes, often quite interesting but marred by some inaccuracies and by superficiality.

485. STEVENSON, PHILIP: "Deporting Jesus". The Nation 143: 67-69 (July 18), 1936.
Background of Labor and Liga Obrera organization in New Mexico, and ensuing struggles.

486. SWADESH, FRANCES LEON: "Property and Kinship in Northern New Mexico". Rocky Mountain Social Science Journal 2/1: 209-214, 1965.
Two related institutions under the impact of change.

487. SWADESH, FRANCES LEON: "The Alianza Movement: Catalyst for Social Change in New Mexico", in Proceedings of the 1968 Annual Spring Meeting of the American Ethnological Society: 162-177. Seattle: University of Washington Press, 1968.
Background of the contemporary land-grant movement.

488. SWADESH, FRANCES LEON: "The Alianza Movement: The Interplay of Social Change and Public Commentary" in Minorities and Politics: 53-84, Henry J. Tobias and Charles E. Woodhouse, eds. Albuquerque: UNM Press, 1969.

489. SWADESH, FRANCES LEON: "The Social and Philosophical Context of Creativity in Hispanic New Mexico". Rocky Mountain Social Science Journal 19/1: 11-18, 1972.
Challenges value orientation analysis of 467.

490. VALDEZ, LUIS and STAN STEINER: Aztlan: An Anthology of Mexican American Literature. New York: Alfred A. Knopf, A Vintage Book, 1972.
Outstanding collection of readings with an excellent introduction by Luis Valdez.

491. VAN DRESSER, PETER: "The Bio-Economic Community: Reflections on a Development Philosophy for a Semiarid Environment", in Indian and Spanish American Adjustments to Arid and Semiarid Environments: 53-74, 1964. Clark S. Knowlton, ed. Lubbock, Texas: Texas Technological College.
Despite its bristling title, a very readable demonstration of the viability of the Hispanic socioeconomic system.

492. VAN DRESSER, PETER: *A Landscape for Humans*. Albuquerque: Biotechnic Press, 1972.
The potential for ecologically guided development in northern New Mexico uplands, harmonious with Hispanic community orientation.

493. WADDISON, JEROLD G.: "Historical Geography of the Middle Puerco Valley, New Mexico". *NMHR 34/4: 248-284, 1959*.
Relationship between settlement patterns and water needs in a changing environment and economy.

494. WALLRICH, WILLIAM: "Auxiliadoras de la Morada". *Southwestern Lore 16/1: 4-10, 1950*.
The role of women in Penitente activities in the San Luis Valley, Colorado.

VI. INTERGROUP RELATIONS

495. BERNSTEIN, HARRY: "Spanish Influence in the United States: Economic Aspects". *Hispanic American Historical Review 18/1: 43-65, 1938*.

496. BRACK, GENE: "Mexican Opinion, American Racism and the War of 1846". *Western Historical Quarterly 1/2: 161-174, 1970*.
While Mexico could not win the war of 1846, public opinion made compromise impossible in the face of U.S. policies of racism and anti-Catholicism.

497. BRAND, DONALD D.: "Southwestern Trade in Shell Products". *American Antiquity 2/4: 300-302, 1937*.
Shells from the Pacific and Gulf of California were elaborated near the sea and traded for pottery of New Mexico Indians in ancient times.

498. ELLIS, FLORENCE H. and EDWIN BACA: "The Apuntes of Father J. B. Ralliere". *NMHR 32/1: 10-15; 32/3: 259-273, 1957*.
Notes by the late priest of Tomé documenting discord with Tomé Grant heirs and religious/cultural rifts caused by Bishop Lamy.

499. FORBES, JACK D.: *Apache, Navajo and Spaniard*. Norman: University of Oklahoma Press, 1960.
Intercultural contact and clash in Colonial times.

500. FRANCIS, E. K.: "Padre Martinez: A New Mexican Myth". NMHR 31/4: 265-289, 1956.
Rifts in the religious life of New Mexico developed when the native clergy was removed after 1850.

501. GAMIO, MANUEL: Race Relations in New Mexico. Chicago: University of Chicago Press, 1930.
Analysis of questionnaires on the causes of racial prejudice.

502. GILLMOR, FRANCES and LOUISA WADE WETHERILL: Traders to the Navajos. Cambirdge: Houghton Mifflin Co., 1952.
The story of the Wetherill family.

503. GUNNERSON, JAMES H.: "Archeological Survey in Northeastern New Mexico". El Palacio 66/5: 346-365, 1959.
Prehistoric contacts between Pueblos and nomadic Indians.

504. HAINES, FRANCIS: "Where Did the Plains Indians Get Their Horses?". AA 40/1: 112-117, 1938.
Horses brought by the Spaniards catalyzed the equestrian-nomadic development of Plains culture. See below and Roe, 1955.

505. HAINES, FRANCIS: "The Northward Spread of Horses Among the Plains Indians". AA 40/3: 429-437, 1938.

506. HEYMAN, MAX L., JR.: "On the Navaho Trail: The Campaign of 1860-61". NMHR 26/1: 44-63, 1951.
Colonel Canby's campaign against the Navajos with two and a half regiments of U.S. troops and "volunteers" who staged counter-raids.

507. HILL, W. W.: "Navaho Trading and Trading Ritual: A Study of Cultural Dynamics". SWJA 4/4: 371-396, 1948.
Stresses Navajo-Pueblo and Navajo-Ute relations, the latter being more cordial than the former in early times.

508. HODGE, FREDERICK W.: "Rites of the Pueblo Indians". El Palacio 18/2: 23-28, 1925.
Broadside at the Indian Rights Association for its meddling in questions of Pueblo ritual seen as "immoral". Records straightfaced Pueblo handling of Anglo mentors.

509. KAPPLER, CHARLES J. (compiler and ed.): Indian Affairs: Laws and Treaties. 3 vols. Washington, D.C.: GPO, 1904.
A basic document on the development of Indian-Government relations. Status of Pueblos as Indians was long disregarded.

510. KELLY, LAWRENCE G.: "The Navaho Indians: Land and Oil". NMHR 38/1: 1-28, 1963.
History of Navajo reservation boundaries from 1868 Treaty to 1934; conflicts between Navajos and large livestock and oil interests.

511. KENNER, CHARLES L.: "The Great New Mexico Cattle Raid, 1872". NMHR 37/4: 243-259, 1963.
Cattle allegedly stolen by Comanches and sold to Hispanos were forcibly seized by a Texas cattle baron and 90 gunmen, causing widespread resentment in New Mexico.

512. LA FARGE, OLIVER: Santa Fe: The Autobiography of a Southwestern Town. Norman: University of Oklahoma Press, 1959.
From the files of the Santa Fe New Mexican, 1863-1953, excerpts emphasize the unique cross-cultural personality of Santa Fe.

513. McKIBBIN, DAVIDSON B.: "Revolt of the Navaho, 1913". NMHR 29/4: 259-289, 1913. Revealing data on Navajo-Anglo relations.

514. MOORHEAD, MAX L.: Jacobo Ugarte and Spanish-Indian Relations in Northern New Spain, 1769-1791. Norman: University of Oklahoma Press, 1968.
Application of Indian policy promulgated by Bernardo de Galvez, 1786 (see Galvez, 1951).

515. MURPHY, LAWRENCE R.: "Reconstruction in New Mexico". NMHR 33/2: 99-115, 1968.
Efforts by Territorial Secretary William F. M. Arny to abolish involuntary servitude for Indians in New Mexico.

516. OPLER, MORRIS E.: "The Influence of Aboriginal Pattern and White Contact on a Recently Introduced Ceremony, the Mescalero Peyote Rite". Journal of American Folklore 49/191-192: 143-166, 1936.
Discovery and use of peyote by the Mescalero Apaches.

517. REED, ERIK K." "Transition to History in the Pueblo Southwest". AA 56/3: 592-599, 1954.
Archeological and documentary evidence of intertribal relations combined in a synthetic analysis.

518. REEVE, FRANK D.: "The Federal Indian Policy in New Mexico". NMHR 13/1: 14-62; 13/3: 146-191; 13/4: 261-313, 1938.
An important contribution with a few inaccuracies.

519. REEVE, FRANK D.: "The Government and the Navaho, 1878-83". NMHR 16: 275-312, 1941.
Sequel to the author's studies of Navajo-Hispanic relations, although published earlier. See Reeve, 1958, 1959, 1960.

520. ROE, FRANK G.: The Indians and the Horse. Norman: University of Oklahoma Press, 1955.
Horses and horsemanship introduced by Spanish settlers affected in a decisive way the culture of many tribes. See Haines, 1938.

521. SIMMONS, MARC: "Governor Anza, the Lipan Apaches and Pecos Pueblo". El Palacio 77/1: 35-40, 1970.
The Lipans, pushed southward by the Comanches, wished to resume their traditional trading relations with Pecos Pueblo in the 1780's.

522. SMYTHE, DONALD S. J.: "John J. Pershing, Frontier Cavalryman". NMHR 38/3: 220-243, 1963.
Includes recreational association with New Mexico Indians.

VII. ARTS AND SKILLS

A. GENERAL

523. BAHTI, TOM: Southwestern Indian Arts and Crafts. Flagstaff, Arizona: K.C. Publications, 1964.
Handsomely illustrates a variety of Indian arts.

524. BOYD, E.: Popular Arts of Colonial New Mexico. Santa Fe: Museum of International Folk Art, 1959. 52 pages illustrated.
Briefly lists the arts and crafts of Colonial New Mexico and how and why they were made.

525. CASSIDY, INA SIZER: "Art and Artists of New Mexico". New Mexico Magazine 16/11: 32-33, 1938.
An informal introduction to some Indian artists: Allan Hauser, Popchalee and Gerald Naylor.

526. DICKEY, ROLAND F.: New Mexico Village Artists. Albuquerque: UNM Press, 1949. Reprinted 1970.
Primarily concerned with Hispanic arts in a historical context, with charming illustrations.

527. GRISWOLD, LESTER: Handicraft. Colorado Springs: Out West Printing and Stationery Company, 1942.
Good sections on Navajo and Hispano weaving, with diagrams and loom set-ups, Navajo silverwork and many other crafts.

528. LEMOS, PEDRO J.: "Marvelous Acoma and its Craftsmen". El Palacio 24/12: 234-244, 1928.
Deals with the then current craft revival at Acoma.

529. NEW MEXICO ASSOCIATION ON INDIAN AFFAIRS: Indian Art Series, Pamphlets 1-13, Santa Fe, N.D.
Beautifully illustrated brief pamphlets on various aspects of Indian art.

530. NEW MEXICO DEPARTMENT OF VOCATIONAL EDUCATION BULLETINS: Mimeo series on "how to make". Santa Fe: n.d.

    Tanning Bulletin
    Spanish Colonial Furniture
    Spanish Colonial Painted Chests
    Tin Craft in New Mexico
    Graphic Standards for Furniture
    New Adaptations from Authentic Examples of Spanish
        Colonial Furniture

The above pamphlets, in mimeograph form, are available in a number of libraries of New Mexico and are unique in their type.

531. TANNER, CLARA LEE: Southwest Indian Craft Arts. Tucson: University of Arizona Press, 1968.
Good general coverage of New Mexico and Arizona with fine illustrations.

532. UNDERHILL, RUTH: Pueblo Crafts. Washington, D.C.: U.S. Indian Service, Education Division, Indian Handicrafts, No. 7, 1945.
Thorough coverage of Pueblo crafts.

533. UNDERHILL, RUTH: Work a Day Life of the Pueblos.
Washington, D.C.: U.S. Indian Service, Education Division, Indian
Life and Customs, No. 4, 1946.
Gives a great deal of information on Pueblo arts and crafts.

B. TEXTILES AND BASKETRY

1. GENERAL

534. DOUGLAS, FREDERICK H.: Southwestern Weaving Materials.
Denver: Denver Art Museum, Department of Indian Art, Leaflet
116, 1953.
A good, brief, regional study.

535. KENT, KATE PECK: The Cultivation and Weaving of Cotton
in the Prehistoric Southwestern United States. Philadelphia:
Transactions of the American Philosophical Society, 47/3, 1957.

536. MASON, OTIS T.: Aboriginal American Basketry. Washington,
D.C.: Smithsonian Institution Annual Report, Part 2, 1902.
Encyclopedic coverage of basketry, including all types in the
Southwest. (Recently reprinted by Rio Grande Press, Glorieta, N.M.).

537. MERA, HARRY P.: The Alfred I. Barton Collection of Southwestern Textiles. Santa Fe: San Vicente Foundation, 1949.
Good, brief survey of Navajo, Pueblo and Rio Grande textile
designs, beautifully illustrated.

538. TILLEY, MARTHA: Three Textile Traditions: Pueblo,
Navajo and Rio Grande. Colorado Springs: The Taylor Museum, 1967.
Handsome recent publication.

2. PUEBLO

539. DOUGLAS, FREDERICK H.: Acoma Pueblo Weaving and Embroidery.
Denver: Denver Art Museum, Department of Indian Art, Leaflet 89,
1939.

540. DOUGLAS, FREDERICK H.: Main Types of Pueblo Cotton Textiles.
Denver: Denver Art Museum, Department of Indian Art, Leaflets
92 and 93, 1940.

541. DOUGLAS, FREDERICK H.: Main Types of Pueblo Woolen Textiles. Denver: Denver Art Museum, Department of Indian Art, Leaflets 94 and 95, 1940.
The three publications listed above are excellent, concise statements.

542. MERA, HARRY P.: Pueblo Indian Embroidery. Santa Fe: Laboratory of Anthropology Memoir No. 4, 1943.
A detailed study of high quality.

543. ROEDIGER, VIRGINIA M.: Ceremonial Costumes of the Pueblo Indians: Their Evolution, Fabrication and Significance in the Prayer Drama. Berkeley and Los Angeles: University of California Press, 1941.
Symbolism of costume elements.

544. SPIER, LESLIE: "Zuñi Weaving Techniques". AA 26/1: 64-85, 1924.
Detailed eyewitness account of steps in spinning and weaving.

3. NAVAJO-APACHE

545. AMSDEN, CHARLES A.: Navaho Weaving, Its Technic and History. Albuquerque: UNM Press, 1949. Recently reprinted by Rio Grande Press, Glorieta, N.M.
A thorough treatment.

546. DUTTON, BERTHA P.: Navajo Weaving Today. Santa Fe: MNM Press, 1963.
Highly recommended.

547. KENT, KATE PECK: Story of Navajo Weaving. Phoenix: Heard Museum of Anthropology and Primitive Arts, 1961.
Historical account of Navajo weaving and diagram of Navajo loom.

548. McNITT, FRANK: "Two Gray Hills -- America's Costliest Rugs". New Mexico Magazine 37/4: 26, 52-53, 1959.
Brief, popular article.

549. MERA, HARRY P.: Navajo Woven Dresses. Santa Fe: Laboratory of Anthropology, General Series, Bulletin No. 14, 1944.

550. MERA, HARRY P.: Navajo Textile Arts. Santa Fe: Laboratory of Anthropology, 1947.
Illustrated series of concise, highly accurate descriptions of individual blankets.

551. REICHARD, GLADYS A.: Spider Woman: A Story of Navajo Weavers and Chanters. New York: Macmillan, 1934. Recently reprinted by Rio Grande Press, Glorieta, N.M.
The place of weaving in Navajo social life.

552. TSCHOPIK, HARRY, JR.: "Navajo Basketry: A Study of Culture Change". AA 42/3: 444-462, 1940.
When this study was made basketmaking had become ringed with so many ritual taboos that most baskets were made only for ceremonial purposes.

4. HISPANO

553. BARKER, RUTH LAUGHLIN: "The Craft of Chimayo". El Palacio 28/6: 161-173, 1930.
Description of Chimayo weavers in Chamber of Commerce style, but the description of Chimayo in 1930 is of historical interest.

554. BLOOM, LANSING B.: "Early Weaving in New Mexico". NMHR 2/3: 228-234, 1927.
Good historical resume, starting with prehistoric Indian cotton textiles. In 1542 sheep were left at Pecos Pueblo by Fray Luis de Escalona. In 1664 employment of Indian women as weavers was forbidden without express permission of the Governor.

555. BOYD, E.: "New Mexican Spanish Textiles". El Palacio 61/5: 134-137, 1954.
Description of the textile collections donated to the State Museum's Spanish Colonial Department, including weaving and embroidery types for different uses.

556. BOYD, E.: "Rio Grande Blankets Containing Handspun Cotton Yarns". El Palacio 71/4: 22-28, 1964.
A description of "naverick" blankets displaying special techniques including ikat dyeing.

557. EMERY, IRENE: "Wool Embroideries of New Mexico: Some Notes on the Stitch Employed". El Palacio 56/11: 340-344, 1949.
The simplest and clearest published statement on the colcha stitch.

558. JAMES, REBECCA: The Colcha Stitch. Santa Fe: Museum of International Folk Art, 1963.
Handsomely illustrated but full understanding requires 557.

559. NEW MEXICO STATE UNIVERSITY: New Mexico Colonial Embroidery. Las Cruces: New Mexico State University Cooperative Extension Service, 1914.
Recently re-issued.

5. ANGLO

560. BIRRELL, VERLA: Textile Arts, A Handbook of Fabric Structure and Design Processes. New York: Harpers, 1959.
Highly recommended as a reference book.

561. BLACK, MARY: New Key to Weaving. Milwaukee: Bruce Publishing Co., 1949.
An excellent general reference.

562. DAVISON, MARGUERITE P.: Handweaver's Pattern Book.
Box 645, Rockville, Md: The Unicorn Press, n.d.
Contains patterns of four harness weaves.

563. DOUGLAS, HARRIET G.: Handweaver's Instruction Manual.
Box 645, Rockville, Md: The Unicorn Press, n.d.
Intended to teach fundamental principles of weaving.

564. EMERY, IRENE: The Primary Structure of Fabrics.
Washington, D.C.: Textile Museum, 1966.
Illustrated classification of weaving techniques in a volume with good bibliography.

565. KILHAM, FRANCES and MARJORIE F. LAMBERT: Fabric for Living.
Santa Fe: Museum of International Folk Art, 1967.
24 pages, illustrated, introducing textile art in man's history.
Brief, concise statements on fibers, spinning, dyes, weaving, etc.

566. THORPE, HEATHER: Handweaver's Work Book. Box 645, Rockville, Md.: The Unicorn Press, n.d.
Comprehensive guide for the new weaver.

C. POTTERY

1. PUEBLO

567. BUNZEL, RUTH L.: The Pueblo Potter: A Study of Creative Imagination in Primitive Art. New York: Columbia University Press, 1929.
For the serious scholar.

568. CHAPMAN, KENNETH M.: "Pottery Decorations of Santo Domingo and Cochiti Pueblos". El Palacio 16/6: 87-93, 1924.
Summary of 30 design elements in all Pueblo pottery decoration, with variety created by combination and arrangement.

569. CHAPMAN, KENNETH M.: "Bird Forms in Zuñi Pottery Decoration". El Palacio 24/1: 23-25, 1928.
Stylized representations exclusive to Zuñi.

570. CHAPMAN, KENNETH M.: The Pottery of Santo Domingo Pueblo. Santa Fe: Laboratory of Anthropology Memoir No. 1, (Second Ed.), 1953.
The definitive work on the pottery of Santo Domingo.

571. CHAPMAN, KENNETH M.: The Pottery of San Ildefonso. Santa Fe: SAR Monograph No. 28, 1970.
Outstanding posthumous publication.

572. DOUGLAS, FREDERICK H.: Pueblo Indian Pottery Making. Denver: Denver Art Museum Pamphlet No. 6, 1940.
Concise and accurate statement.

573. GUTHE, CARL E.: Pueblo Pottery Making, A Study at the Village of San Ildefonso. New Haven: Yale University Press, Papers of the Phillips Academy Southwest Expedition No. 2, 1925.
Report on the study that revived Pueblo pottery making.

574. HARLOW, FRANCIS H.: Historic Pueblo Indian Pottery. Santa Fe: MNM Press, PH 6, 1967.
A run-through of designs characteristic of different Pueblos.

575. HARLOW, FRANCES H. and JOHN V. YOUNG: Contemporary Pueblo Indian Pottery. Santa Fe: MNM Press, PH 5, 1965.
Handy guide for the prospective buyer.

576. KIDDER, ALFRED V. and ANNA O. SHEPARD: The Pottery of Pecos.
New Haven: Yale University Press for the Phillips Academy, Vol. 1
(1931), Vol. 2 (1936).
A comprehensive and beautifully illustrated study.

577. LAMBERT, MARJORIE: Pueblo Indian Pottery: Materials,
Tools, Techniques. Santa Fe: MNM Popular Series, Pamphlet No. 5,
1966.
Brief but thorough treatment of pottery making.

578. MARRIOTT, ALICE: Maria: The Potter of San Ildefonso.
Norman: University of Oklahoma Press, 1950.
In the form of a biography, much information on Pueblo pottery
and Pueblo life in general are provided.

579. MERA, HARRY P.: The "Rain Bird": A Study in Pueblo Design.
Santa Fe: Laboratory of Anthropology Memoir No. 2, 1937.
A classic scholarly analysis of design.

580. MERA, HARRY P.: Style Trends of Pueblo Pottery in the
Rio Grande and Little Colorado Cultural Areas from the 16th to
the 19th Century. Santa Fe: Laboratory of Anthropology Memoir
No. 3, 1939.
A must for serious students of Pueblo art.

581. WARREN, HELENE: "Tonque". El Palacio 76/2: 36-42, 1969.
This archeological site is the principal source of early Rio
Grande glaze pottery.

582. WORMINGTON, H. M. and ARMINTA NEAL: The Story of Pueblo
Pottery. Denver: Museum of Natural History, Pictorial No. 2, 1956.
Fine photographs of pots from past and present with clear
explanation of how they were made.

2. NAVAJO-APACHE

583. TSCHOPIK, HARRY, JR.: "Taboo as a Possible Factor in the
Obsolescence of Navajo Pottery and Basketry". AA 40/2: 257-262,
1938. See 552.

3. HISPANO

584. LISTER, FLORENCE C. and ROBERT H.: "Majolica: Ceramic Link Between Old World and New". El Palacio 76/2: 3-15, 1969.
A general article on the only non-Indian ware used in Spanish Colonial times.

585. PLOWDEN, WILLIAM W., JR.: "Spanish and Mexican Majolica Found in New Mexico". El Palacio 65/6: 212-219, 1958.
These wares are important for dating, also for historical reconstruction.

586. SNOW, DAVID H.: "The Chronological Position of Mexican Majolica in the Southwest". El Palacio 72/1: 25-35, 1965.
Classification of Early, Transitional and Late wares found in New Mexico.

4. ANGLO

587. KENNY, JOHN B.: The Complete Book of Pottery Making. Philadelphia and New York: Chilton Books, 1963.
A "how to" book without reference to the Southwest.

588. KENNY, JOHN B.: Ceramic Design. Philadelphia and New York: Chilton Books, 1963.
A general book of design.

D. PICTORIAL AND DECORATIVE ARTS

1. GENERAL

589. ADAIR, JOHN: Navajo and Pueblo Silversmiths. Norman: University of Oklahoma Press, 1946.
A comparative work.

590. BENNETT, EDNA MAE: Turquoise and the Indian. Denver: Sage Books, 1966.
Regionwide study with maps of mining districts; physical description of area; reports by Spaniards; contemporary jewelry and pawn; turquoise in Indian legend and archeology; bibliography.

591. DUNN, DOROTHY: <u>American Indian Painting of the Southwest and Plains Area</u>. Albuquerque: UNM Press, 1968.
Good general work of recent vintage.

592. HODGE, FREDERICK W.: "How Old is Southwestern Indian Silverwork?", <u>El Palacio 25/14-17: 224-232, 1928</u>.
Archeology and Ethnohistory combined.

593. HODGE, FREDERICK W.: <u>Decorative Art of the Southwestern Indians</u>. New York: Dover Publications, 1936. Reprinted 1961.
Covers the field.

594. HUNT, W. BEN: <u>Indian Silversmithing</u>. Milwaukee: The Bruce Publishing Company, 1960.
A "how to" book prepared for the Boy Scouts of America, with many sketches of designs.

595. KIRK, RUTH FALKENBURG: <u>Southwestern Indian Jewelry</u>. Santa Fe: SAR Papers, No. 38, 1945.

596. MERA, HARRY P.: <u>Indian Silverwork of the Southwest</u>. Globe, Arizona: Dale Stuart King, Publ., 1960. Illustrated.

597. SCHAAFSMA, POLLY: <u>Rock Art in the Navajo Reservoir District</u>. Santa Fe: MNM Papers in Anthropology, No. 7, 1963.
Petroglyphs and pictographs, now submerged by Navajo Reservoir, are discussed and illustrated.

598. SCHAAFSMA, POLLY: <u>Southwest Indian Pictographs and Petroglyphs</u>. Santa Fe: MNM Press, 1965.
Popular pamphlet, scholarly but readable.

599. SCHAAFSMA, POLLY: <u>Early Navaho Rock Paintings and Carvings</u>. Santa Fe: Museum of Navaho Ceremonial Art, 1966.
Booklet describing the art of Navajo Indians of Governador Canyon and Canyon Largo under the influence of Pueblo Indians who lived with them after 1680 Revolt.

600. SCHAAFSMA, POLLY: "The Los Lunas Petroglyphs". <u>El Palacio 75/2: 13-24, 1968</u>.
A brief, well illustrated article with discussion of how to classify Pueblo rock art.

601. SCHAAFSMA, POLLY: Indian Rock Art in New Mexico.
Santa Fe: State Planning Office and UNM Press, 1973.
Authoritative survey with superb photographs, some in color.

602. SIDES, DOROTHY SMITH: Decorative Art of the Southwestern Indians. New York: Dover Publishing Co, 1961.
A general work of good quality.

603. TANNER, CLARA LEE: Southwest Indian Painting. Tucson: University of Arizona Press, 1957.

604. TANNER, CLARA LEE: "Contemporary Southwest Indian Silver". The Kiva 25/3: 1-22, 1960.
Both this listing and the one above are widely used.

2. PUEBLO

605. CHAPMAN, KENNETH M.: "A Feather Symbol of the Ancient Pueblos". El Palacio 23/21: 526-540, 1927.
Eagle tail feather designs are found in pictographs and in ceramic design, as conventionalized symbolic forms.

606. COLTON, HAROLD S.: Hopi Kachina Dolls. Albuquerque: UNM Press, 1949. Reprinted 1959.
Well illustrated, explains many kachina types.

607. DUTTON, BERTHA: Sun Father's Way: The Kiva Murals of Kuaua. Albuquerque: UNM Press, 1963.
Symbolic design of an archeological religious center, explained by a contemporary Indian from a different Pueblo grouping.
Fine illustrations.

608. ELLIS, FLORENCE H. and LAURENS HAMMACK: "The Inner Sanctum of Feather Cave, A Mogollon Sun and Earth Shrine Linking Mexico and the Southwest". American Antiquity 33/1: 25-44, 1968.
A site in Lincoln County abandoned in late 14th century, with special design elements and art style.

609. HILL, GERTRUDE F.: "Turquoise and the Zuñi Indian". The Kiva 12/4: 45-52, 1947.

610. PARSONS, ELSIE CLEWS (ed. by Esther Goldfrank): Isleta Paintings. Washington, D.C.: BAE Bulletin No. 18, 1962.
A monumental posthumous work with exquisite paintings of ceremonials redone by an Isleta artist.

611. SIMS, AGNES C.: San Cristobal Petroglyphs. Santa Fe: Southwest Editions, 1950.
Rubbings taken from a cliff face near Galisteo with brief explanation.

612. WRIGHT, BARTON and EVELYN ROAT: This is a Hopi Kachina. Flagstaff: Museum of Northern Arizona, 1965.
Popular but scholarly explanation of some kachina figures.

3. NAVAJO APACHE

613. HILL, GERTRUDE F.: "The Art of the Navajo Silversmith". The Kiva 2/5: 17-20, 1937.

614. HILL, GERTRUDE F.: "The Use of Turquoise Among the Navajo". The Kiva 4/3: 11-14, 1938.

615. MATTHEWS, WASHINGTON: "Navajo Silversmiths". BAE Second Annual Report: 167-178, 1883.
An article of much historical interest.

616. WOODWARD, ARTHUR: A Brief History of Navajo Silversmithing. Flagstaff: Museum of Northern Arizona, Bulletin No. 14, 1938.
Concise and authoritative.

617. WYMAN, LELAND C.: Navajo Indian Painting: Symbolism, Artistry and Psychology. Boston: Boston University Press, 1959.

4. HISPANO

618. BOYD, E.: "A New Mexican Retablo and its Mexican Prototype", El Palacio 56/12: 355-357, 1949.
A print of the image of "Our Lady of the Little Village" from Queretaro inspired a New Mexico religious artist.

619. BOYD, E.: "Santos of the Southwest". House and Garden 102/6: 91-92, 1952.

620. BOYD, E.: "The Crucifix in Santero Art". El Palacio 60/3: 112-115, 1953.
Stylistic variations in the depiction of the crucifix.

621. BOYD, E.: New Mexico Santos. Santa Fe: School of American Research, Department of Spanish Colonial Art, Leaflet No. 1, 1953.
A concise statement.

622. BOYD, E.: New Mexico Santos: How to Name Them. Santa Fe: International Folk Art Foundation, 1966.
Contains much iconographic information.

623. BOYD, E.: The New Mexico Santero. Santa Fe: MNM Press, 1969.
A recent booklet including the latest data on individual santeros.

624. COKE, VAN DEREN: "A Saint-Carver in New Mexico". Art in America 1: 124-127, 1965.
Introduction to a contemporary santero, Jose Mondragon of Cordova.

625. ESPINOSA, GILBERTO: "New Mexican Santos". NM Quarterly 6/3: 181-189, 1936.
The author is the owner of an important santo collection.

626. ESPINOSA, JOSE E.: Saints in the Valleys. Albuquerque: UNM Press (Revised Ed.), 1967.
Interesting and beautifully illustrated description focussed on the Gilberto Espinosa collection.

627. HOUGLAND, WILLARD: Santos: A Primitive American Art. Foreword by Donald Bear. New York: Jan Klejkamp and Ellis Monroe, 1946.
A work of importance for art collectors.

628. MILLS, GEORGE: People of the Saints. Colorado Springs: The Taylor Museum, n.d.
Information on the art and the cultural environment of santeros.

629. SHALKOP, ROBERT L.: Wooden Saints. Colorado Springs: The Taylor Museum, 1967.
A recent work, well written and illustrated.

630. SHALKOP, ROBERT L.: <u>Arroyo Hondo: The Folk Art of a New Mexican Village</u>. Colorado Springs: The Taylor Museum, 1969.
Depiction of a recently recognized distinctive style.

631. WENHAM, EDWARD: "Spanish American Silver of New Mexico". <u>International Studio 99/40, 1931</u>.

632. WENHAM, EDWARD: "The Colonial Silver of Early Spanish America". <u>The Fine Arts 18/4, 1932</u>.
A general study, which should be read jointly with the preceding work.

633. WILDER, M. A. and E. BREITENBACH: <u>Santos: The Religious Folk Art of New Mexico</u>. Colorado Springs: The Taylor Museum, 1943.

5. ANGLO

634. COKE, VAN DEREN: <u>Taos and Santa Fe: The Artist's Environment 1882-1942</u>. Albuquerque: UNM Press, 1963.
Arranged chronologically, the author's penetrating study gives major attention to more than three-score men and women who have made distinctive contributions to American art.

635. LUHAN, MABEL DODGE: <u>Taos and its Artists</u>. New York: Duell, Sloan and Pierce, 1947.
Now out of print. Includes photos of artists and their work with a text by Mabel Dodge Luhan about the artists whom she knew as friends.

636. MEIGS, JOHN, ed.: <u>Peter Hurd: The Lithographs</u>. Lubbock: Baker Gallery Press, 1968.
Technical explanation of Hurd's lithographs and reproductions. Photos of the artist at work.

637. NEW MEXICO ARTISTS: <u>Guest Artist Series from the New Mexico Quarterly, Series 3</u>. Albuquerque: UNM Press, 1949.
Eight important art critiques, with reproductions of each artist's works. Artists included are: John Sloan, Ernest Blumenschein, Gustave Baumann, Kenneth Adams, Adja Yunkers, Raymond Johnson, Peter Hurd and Howard Cook.

638. SLOAN, JOHN: <u>The Gist of Art</u>. New York: American Artists Group, 1939.
Principles and practice in classroom and studio recorded with the assistance of Helen Farr. Many illustrations of Sloan's works, including those in the collection of the Museum of New Mexico.

639. TAFT, ROBERT: <u>Artists and Illustrators of the Old West, 1850-1900</u>. New York: Charles Scribner's Sons, 1953.
Much of the book was originally published as a series of articles in the Kansas Historical Quarterly, telling of the artists whose paintings documented the westward surge of settlement.

640. WALTERS, FRANK: <u>Leon Gaspard</u>. Flagstaff: Northland Press, 1964.
Biographical study of the painter whose life started in Russia, whose travels and work included Mongolia, Tibet, Siberia and France, ending in Taos. Color reproductions of his work.

VII-E. <u>ARCHITECTURE AND HOUSE INTERIORS</u>

1. <u>GENERAL</u>

641. BUNTING, BAINBRIDGE and JOHN P. CONRON: "The Architecture of Northern New Mexico". <u>New Mexico Architecture 8/9-10 (entire Sept.-Oct. number), 1966</u>.
Excellent article, profusely illustrated with photos, including seven sections: 1. Architectural Background, 2. The Morada, 3. A Village and its Church: Las Trampas, 4. Picurís Indian Pueblo, 5. Chimayó, 6. El Santuario de Nuestro Señor de Esquípula, 7. Santa Fé.

642. FARMER, MALCOLM F.: "A Suggested Topology for Defensive Structures of the Southwest". <u>SWJA 13/3: 249-266, 1957</u>.
A variety of Indian defensive systems, some with much wider distribution than the Southwest, summarized from archeological and ethnohistoric data.

643. HESSELDEN, LOUIS G.: "New Mexico Architecture". <u>NMQR 13/3: 326-332, 1943</u>.
Brief general treatment.

2. PUEBLO

644. CHAPMAN, KENNETH M.: "Stone Wall Construction in Ancient Pueblos and Cliff Dwellings". El Palacio 23/19: 479-485, 1927.
Typological study.

645. JUDD, NEIL M.: The Architecture of Pueblo Bonito. Washington, D.C.: Smithsonian Miscellaneous Collection 147/1, 1964.
Major work with excellent photos of the largest and most famous of Chaco Canyon pueblos, occupied 900-1100 A.D. Text may be too technical for the general reader.

646. MAUZY, WAYNE: "Architecture for the Ancients". New Mexico Magazine 15/2: 12-13, 1937.
Discusses use of adobes in Indian architecture both before and after Spanish conquest.

647. MAUZY, WAYNE: "Architecture of the Pueblos". El Palacio 42/4-6: 21-30, 1937.
Prehispanic and posthispanic methods of making adobe structures.

648. MINDELEFF, VICTOR: A Study of Pueblo Architecture: Tusayan and Cibola. BAE 8th Annual Report for 1886-1887, Washington, D.C.: GPO, 1887.

3. NAVAJO-APACHE

649. CORBETT, JOHN M.: "Navajo House Types". El Palacio 47/5: 97-107, 1940.
In Chaco Canyon, square stone houses and square timber hogans were predominant in a survey of 150 houses.

650. MINDELEFF, COSMOS: "Houses and House Dedication of the Navajos". Scientific American 82: 233-234, 1950.

4. HISPANO

651. ADAMS, ELEANOR B.: "The Chapel and Cofradia of Our Lady of Light in Santa Fe". NMHR 22/4: 327-341, 1947.
Description based on the Dominguez 1776 report.

652. AHLBORN, RICHARD E.: The Penitente Moradas of Abiquiu.
Washington, D.C.: Smithsonian Press, Contributions from the
Museum of History and Technology No. 63, 1968.
Descriptive and historical coverage with great detail both in
illustrations and references.

653. BORHEGYI, STEPHEN F. DE: El Santuario de Chimayó.
Santa Fe: The Spanish Colonial Arts Society, Inc., 1956.
Concise history of the shrine and cult of Our Lord of
Esquípulas in Guatemala and New Mexico, with description of both
the exterior and interior of the Santuario.

654. BOYD, E.: "Fireplaces and Stoves in Colonial New Mexico".
El Palacio 65/6: 219-224, 1958.
Information on home interiors, both Hispanic and Pueblo, including
"estufas" for cooking, "hornos" for outdoor baking and the
"fogon" -- "de campana" (bell shaped) and "de padercito" (in the
wall).

655. BUNTING, BAINBRIDGE, ET AL: Taos Adobes. Santa Fe: MNM
Monograph No. 10, 1964.
Meticulous descriptions of a few fine Territorial houses and
historical typology of structural details, with photos and
diagrams.

656. ELLIS, BRUCE: The Historic Palace of the Governors.
Santa Fe: MNM Press, 1968.
A popular-priced Museum guide with a map of former Palace layout.

657. HEWETT, EDGAR L. and REGINALD G. FISHER: Mission Monuments
of New Mexico. Albuquerque: UNM and SAR, 1943.
Historical and archeological orientation, useful with 659.

658. JONES, HESTER: "Uses of Wood by the Spanish Colonists in
New Mexico". NMHR 7/3: 273-291, 1932.
The kinds of wood available, where obtained and how used in
architecture, furniture and finish, statues and implements.
Illustrated and described in historical context.

659. KUBLER, GEORGE C.: The Religious Architecture of New
Mexico in the Colonial Period and since the American Occupation.
Colorado Springs: The Taylor Museum, 1940.
The best coverage, clearest diagramming and most sumptuous
illustrations on this topic.

660. MATHEWS, TRUMAN: "Architecture with a Past". New Mexico Magazine 30/5: 18-19, 43, 45, 1952.
Brief, popular description of Colonial and Territorial houses fast disappearing in New Mexico.

661. SIMMONS, MARC: "Settlement Patterns and Village Plans in Colonial New Mexico". Journal of the West 8/1: 7-21, 1969.
Variant settlement patterns in historical transition.

5. ANGLO

662. ALLER, PAUL and DORIS: Build Your Own Adobe. Stanford: Stanford University Press, 1946.
Good "how to" information.

663. HUBBELL, ELBERT: Earth Brick Construction. Chilocco: U.S. Office of Indian Affairs, Education Division, 1943.

664. MATHEWS, TRUMAN: "Patterned from the Past". New Mexico Magazine 17/5: 22-23, 36, 38-39, 1939.
Coverage of the transition from Indian to Hispanic structures as determined by different life styles.

665. MATHEWS, TRUMAN: "Adobe...in One Easy Lesson". New Mexico Magazine 24/5: 11-14, 1946.

666. McGARR, CUVIER: "Your Adobe Casa". New Mexico Magazine 26/4: 11-15, 43-46, 1948.
Modern adaptations of traditional adobe construction.

667. MORLEY, SYLVANUS G.: "Development of the Santa Fe Style of Architecture". Old Santa Fe 2/3: 278-301, 1915.
Historical treatment of the topic.

668. NEUBAUER, L.W.: Adobe Construction Methods. Berkeley: University of California Agricultural Publications, n.d.

669. U.S. DEPARTMENT OF COMMERCE: Handbook for Building Homes of Earth, PB No. 179-237, n.d.
Springfield, Virginia: Clearinghouse for Federal Scientific and Technical Information.

670. VIERRA, CARLOS: "Our Native Architecture in its Relation to Santa Fe". El Palacio 4/1: 5-11, 1917.
An early argument for preserving the architectural integrity of Santa Fe.

VII-F. MUSIC, DANCE, DRAMA, RITUAL AND POETRY

1. GENERAL

671. ASTROV, MARGOT ed. and introd.: The Winged Serpent: An Anthrology of American Indian Prose and Poetry. New York: The John Day Company, 1946.
Sections III and IV contain fine southwestern examples.

672. BAHTI, TOM: Southwestern Indian Ceremonials. Las Vegas: K.C. Publications, 1971. (second printing).
Authoritative and sumptuously illustrated.

673. CONCHA, JOSEPH L.: Lonely Deer: Poems by a Pueblo Indian Boy. Taos: Red Willow Society, 1969.
A slender volume of beautiful short poems.

674. DOCKSTADER, FREDERICK: The Kachina and the White Man: The Influences of the White Culture on the Hopi Kachina Cult. Bloomfield Hills, Mich.: Cranbrook Institute of Science, Bull. No. 35, 1954. (Out of print but available from the Museum of the American Indian.)
Contains information on ceremonial changes at Zuñi as well as among the Hopi.

675. FERGUSSON, ERNA: Dancing Gods: Indian Ceremonials of New Mexico and Arizona. Albuquerque: UNM Press, 1961.
Originally published in 1931, now available in paperback reprint. Very readable account of dance-dramas and legends of Rio Grande Pueblos, Zuñis, Hopis, Navajos and Apaches.

676. McALLISTER, DAVID P.: Indian Music in the Southwest. Colorado Springs: The Taylor Museum, 1961.
Good, brief illustrated introduction for the layman.

677. UNDERHILL, RUTH: "Ceremonial Patterns in the Southwest". Memoirs of the American Ethnological Society 13: 1-62, 1948.
Area-wide uniformities and variations.

678. VAN STONE, MARY R.: "The Matachina Dance". El Palacio 38/1-2: 10-12, 1935.
Brief general description.

679. WARREN, NINA OTERO: Old Spain in Our Southwest. New York: Harcourt Brace, 1936.
A popular book tracing New Mexican Hispanic fiestas, songs, etc. back to roots in Spain.

2. PUEBLO

680. ANONYMOUS: "Comanche Dance at San Ildefonso". El Palacio 10/4: 5-7, 1921.

681. ANONYMOUS: "The Animal Dance at San Ildefonso". El Palacio 24/7-8: 119-122, 1928.
The above two titles provide concise descriptions.

682. BUNZEL, RUTH: "Introduction to Zuñi Ceremonialsim". BAE 47th Annual Report: 467-544, 1932.
For serious students.

683. DEHUFF, ELIZABETH WILLIS: "Indians and Irony". El Palacio 22/12: 261-264, 1927.
Farcical reenactment of the coming of Spaniards and Anglo Americans in dramas for fun put on by the Koshares. See 685.

684. DEHUFF, ELIZABETH WILLIS: "December Indian Dances". New Mexico Magazine 10/11: 14-15, 45-47, 1932.
The Matachine and Shalako illustrations make this article worth examining.

685. DOZIER, THOMAS: "Historical Pageantry at Santa Clara Pueblo". El Palacio 10/12: 3-5, 1921.
Reminiscences on a December 1893 farcical reenactment of the arrival of Anglo-American troops, Navajo raids and the coming of Ute warriors to the rescue. Compare with 683.

686. DUTTON, BERTHA and MIRIAM A. MARMON: The Laguna Calendar. UNM Anthropological Series, Bulletin No. 1/2, 1936.
Method of counting days and years, with a list of yearly ceremonies.

687. KURATH, GERTRUDE P.: "Plaza Circuits of Tewa Indian Dances". El Palacio 65/1: 16-26, 1958.
Observations on the counter-clockwise and cardinal directional regularities of Pueblo dances.

688. KURATH, GERTRUDE P. with ANTONIO GARCIA: Music and Dance of the Tewa Pueblos. Santa Fe: MNM Press, 1970.
An important, unique work for the serious student.

689. LANGE, CHARLES: "The Feast Day at Zia Pueblo, New Mexico". Texas Journal of Science 4/1:19-26, 1952.

690. LANGE, CHARLES: "Tablita or Corn Dances of the Rio Grande Pueblo Indians". Texas Journal of Science 9/1: 59-74, 1957.
The above two titles provide thorough, brief descriptions.

691. PARSONS, ELSIE CLEWS and RALPH BEALS: "The Sacred Clowns of the Pueblo and Mayo-Yaqui Indians". AA 36/4: 491-544, 1934.
Exploration of a ceremonial tradition of the Greater Southwest.

3. NAVAJO-APACHE

692. CHALAPI: Navajo Indian Peoms: Translations from the Navajo and Other Peoms as told to Hilda Faunce Wetherill. New York: Vantage Press, 1952.

693. GOODWIN, GRENVILLE: "A Comparison of Navajo and White Mountain Apache Ceremonial Forms and Categories". SWJA 1/4: 498-506, 1945.
Navajo ceremonial patterns, while more complex than Apache, are not as complex as they seem.

694. KLUCKHOHN, CLYDE: "Participation in Ceremonials in a Navajo Community". AA 40/3: 359-369, 1938.
During a 6-month period about 20% of annual income was spent on the average for ceremonials, as a focal point in Navajo society.

695. KLUCKHOHN, CLYDE and LELAND C. WYMAN: <u>An Introduction to Navajo Chant Practice, with an Account of the Behaviors Observed in Four Chants</u>. AAAM 53, 1940.
A companion work to 705. Detailed observations.

696. MATTHEWS, WASHINGTON: "The Mountain Chant, A Navajo Ceremony" with original text and translation of songs. <u>BAE 5th Annual Report: 385-467, 1887</u>. Recently reprinted by Rio Grande Press, Glorieta, N.M.
The Bear Ceremony, carefully recorded for the serious student.

697. MATTHEWS, WASHINGTON: <u>The Night Chant: A Navajo Ceremony</u>. New York: AMNH Memoirs, Vol. 6, 1902.
During this 9-day ceremony, children are initiated.

698. NEWCOMB, FRANC J.: "Symbols in Sand". <u>New Mexico Magazine 14/12: 24-25, 37-38, 1936</u>.
Focus on description of the Male Shooting Chant, with illustrations.

699. NEWCOMB, FRANC J.: "How the Navajo Adopt Rites". <u>El Palacio 46/2: 25-27, 1939</u>.
Compare with 446. Borrowing of a Laguna ritual into a minor ceremony.

700. NICHOLS, DAN: "Mescalero Apache Girls' Puberty Ceremony". <u>El Palacio 46/9: 193-204, 1939</u>.
Detailed explanation by a Mescalero author.

701. OPLER, MORRIS E.: "The Sacred Clowns of the Chiricahua and Mescalero Indians". <u>El Palacio 44/10-12: 75-79, 1938</u>.
A reflection of the Greater Southwestern Tradition explored by Parsons and Beals, 1934, and Underhill, 1948.

702. OPLER, MORRIS E.: "Adolescence Rites of the Jicarilla". <u>El Palacio 49/2: 25-38, 1942</u>.
Information as recounted and interpreted by Jicarillas.

703. REICHARD, GLADYS A.: "Distinctive Features of Navajo Religion". <u>SWJA 1/2: 199-220, 1945</u>.
A discussion article comparing Navajo and Pueblo religious philosophy and practice.

704. WOODS, BETTY: "Jicarilla Fiesta". <u>New Mexico Magazine</u> <u>19/9: 16-17, 37, 39, 41, 1941</u>.
Superficial and tourist-oriented description of the Stone Lake September festival, interesting because based on observations long time ago.

705. WYMAN, LELAND C. and CLYDE KLUCKHOHN: <u>Navaho Classification</u> <u>of Their Song Ceremonials</u>. AAAM No. 59, 1938.
Very scholarly but interesting for those who seek cross-cultural insight. A companion work to 695.

4. HISPANO

706. CAMPA, ARTHUR L.: "Religious Spanish Folk-Drama in New Mexico". <u>NMQR 2/1: 3-13, 1932</u>.
Deals with two play cycles: from the Creation to the Fall of Lucifer (Adan y Eva, Cain y Abel, Lucifer y San Miguel) and the Christmas Cycle (El Coloquio de San Jose, El Auto del Niño Dios, El Auto de los Reyes Magos, El Auto del Niño Perdido).

707. CAMPA, ARTHUR L.: <u>Spanish Folk Song in the Southwest</u>.
Albuquerque: UNM Modern Language Series, Bulletin No. 4, 1933.

708. CAMPA, ARTHUR L.: <u>Spanish Religious Folk Theatre in the</u> <u>Spanish Southwest</u>, First Cycle, Second Cycle. Albuquerque: UNM Press, 1934.
An expansion of 706.

709. CAMPA, ARTHUR L.: <u>Los Comanches: A New Mexico Folk Drama</u>.
Albuquerque: UNM Modern Language Series Bulletin No. 7/6, 1942.

710. CAMPA, ARTHUR L.: <u>Spanish Folk Poetry in New Mexico</u>.
Albuquerque: UNM Press, 1946.
An outstanding collection.

711. ESPINOSA, AURELIO M.: <u>Los Comanches</u>. Albuquerque: UNM Modern Language Series, Bulletin No. 1/1, 1907. Translated by Gilberto Espinosa, New Mexico Quarterly, May, 1931: 133-146.
A regional folk drama in Spanish, reflecting life in New Mexico.

712. LUCERO-WHITE, AURORA: <u>Los Hispanos</u>. Denver: Sage Books, Inc., 1947.
Brief description of Hispanic musical dramas and fiestas.

713. MAREAU, HELENE; AURORA LUCERO-WHITE and EUNICE HAUSKINS: Folk Dances of the Spanish Colonials of New Mexico. Santa Fe: Privately Printed, 1940.

714. ORTEGA, PETER RIBERA: Christmas in Old Santa Fe. Santa Fe: Piñon Publishing Company, 1961.

715. ORTEGA, PETER RIBERA: "Las Posadas". El Palacio 75/4: 5-9, 1968.
Description of pre-Christmas fiestas and observances.

716. RAEL, JUAN B.: The New Mexican Alabado. Stanford: Stanford University Press, 1951.
The standard work published to date on the religious vocal music of New Mexico.

717. RAEL, JUAN B.: "More Light on the Origin of Los Pastores". NM Folklore Record 6: 1-6, 1951-1952.
The New Mexico versions correspond roughly with versions in various Mexican towns, both probably originating in the same Mexican source.

718. ROBB, JOHN D.: Hispanic Folk Songs of New Mexico. Albuquerque: UNM Press, 1954.
Background work with bibliography. Music of a number of songs, with words in Spanish and English.

719. SEDILLO, MELA: Mexican and New Mexican Folkdances. Albuquerque: UNM Press, 1950.
Describes the dances and the occasions on which they are performed.

720. STARK, RICHARD B., with T. M. PEARCE and RUBEN COBOS: Music of the Spanish Folk Plays in New Mexico. Santa Fe:MNM Press, 1969.
The music of 17 versions of Los Pastores and a musical version of El Niño Perdido. Two texts of Los Pastores and a commentary on poetic forms by Ruben Cobos.

VII-G. STORYTELLING, MYTHS AND HEALING

1. GENERAL

721. CASSIDY, INA SIZER: "Folklore in New Mexico". NM Folklore Record 11: 3-6, 1947-1948.
A comparison of Pueblo and Navajo folktales with those of Hispanos and Anglos in terms of leading themes, style, etc.

722. VOGEL, VIRGIL J: American Indian Medicine. Norman: University of Oklahoma Press, 1970.

> NOTE: THERE ARE ARTICLES TOO NUMEROUS TO LIST, RELATING TO NEW MEXICO FOLKLORE, MYTHOLOGY AND FOLK MEDICINE, IN THE CALIFORNIA FOLKLORE QUARTERLY, THE NEW MEXICO QUARTERLY AND THE TEXAS FOLKLORE SOCIETY PUBLICATIONS.

2. PUEBLO

723. APPLEGATE, FRANK G.: Indian Stories from the Pueblos. Glorieta, NM: Rio Grande Press (reprint), 1972.
Stories retold, with illustrations, in popular style.

724. BENEDICT, RUTH: Tales of the Cochiti Indians. BAE Bulletin No. 98., 1931.

725. BROWN, MARIE HAMILTON: "Tales of Isleta". NM Quarterly 3/1: 9-17, 1933.

726. BROWN, MARIE HAMILTON: "Tales of Isleta". NM Quarterly 4: 281-290, 1934.

727. CATA, REGINA ALBARADO DE and THELMA CLARKE: Runaway Boy (Raton Jemez). Albuquerque: Clarke Industries, 1969.
A story with a moral, about a lazy boy, for children of elementary school age.

728. DEHUFF, ELIZABETH WILLIS: "Pueblo Myths and Legends". El Palacio 11/8: 98-99, 1921. An enjoyable comparison of Zia and San Juan stories, also paralleled among the Hopis, about the fate of the witch wife.

729. DEHUFF, ELIZABETH WILLIS: Tay-Tay's Tales. New York: Harcourt, 1922.
A re-telling of Pueblo folk tales, enjoyable for children.

730. FOX, ROBIN: "Witchcraft and Clanship in Cochiti Healing". In Magic, Faith and Healing, Ari Kiev, ed., Glencoe, California: Glencoe Press, 1964.

731. STIRLING, MATTHEW W.: Origin Myth of Acoma and Other Records. BAE Bulletin No. 135, 1942.
For the serious student.

732. TYLER, HAMILTON A.: Pueblo Gods and Myths. Norman: University of Oklahoma Press, 1964.
A general overview.

733. VELARDE, PABLITA: Old Father, The Story Teller. Globe, Arizona: Dale Stuart King Press, 1960.
Legends told to the author by her Santa Clara grandfather and great-grandfather.

734. WATERS, FRANK: The Book of the Hopi. New York: Viking Press, 1963.
Available in paperback, profusely illustrated from prehistoric kiva murals, the origin myth of the Hopis as told by certain elders.

735. WHITE, LESLIE A.: A Comparative Study of Keresan Medicine Societies. Proceedings of the 23rd International Congress of Americanists. Lancaster, Penna: The Science Press Printing Company, 1928.

736. ZUNI PEOPLE, THE: The Zunis: Self-Portrayals: Albuquerque: UNM Press, 1972.
Forty-six stores from the oral tradition, translated by Alvina Quam.

3. NAVAJO-APACHE

737. ASTROV, MARGOT: "The Concept of Motion as the Psychological Leitmotif of Navajo Life and Literature". Journal of American Folklore 63/247: 45-56, 1950.
A remarkable insight into Navajo culture, through a recurrent theme.

738. BAILEY, FLORA L.: "Navaho Women and the Sudatory". AA 43/3: 484-485, 1941.
A brief communication about the sweat-house in the maintenance and restoration of health.

739. BOURKE, JOHN G.: The Medicine Men of the Apaches. Glorieta, NM: Rio Grande Press.
Reprint of observations in the 1880's originally published in the BAE Ninth Annual Report.

740. HAILE, FATHER BERARD: "Navaho Chantways and Ceremonials". AA 40/4: 639-652, 1938. Careful examination of Navajo definitions of words repeatedly used to describe certain aspects of curing ceremonials.

741. HAILE, FATHER BERARD: Origin Legend of the Navaho Enemy Way. New Haven: Yale University Publications in Anthropology No. 17, 1938.
Text, translation and explanation of a major ceremonial complex to cure effects of contact with dead enemies.

742. HAILE, FATHER BERARD: "A Note on the Navaho Visionary". AA 42/2: 359, 1940.
A brief communication on visions as sources of power which created ceremonials, comparing legend with actual instances.

743. HAILE, FATHER BERARD: Starlore Among the Navaho. Santa Fe: Museum of Navaho Ceremonial Art, 1947.
How the Navajos identify constellations, the myths concerning their origin and the ceremonies in which they are depicted; also the use of starlore for divination of disease and the ceremonies needed to cure it.

744. HAWLEY, FLORENCE M.: "Navajo Night". New Mexico Magazine 20/1: 22, 33-35, 1942.
Recollections of a night spent encamped with Navajos, during Enemy Way ceremonial.

745. HILL, W. W.: "The Hand Trembling Ceremony of the Navajo". El Palacio 38/12-14: 65-68, 1935.
For diagnosis of illness of unknown causes, for locating lost or stolen property, water or persons, or for predicting the outcome of a war raid or hunting venture.

746. HILL, W. W.: "Navajo Rites for Dispelling Insanity and Delirium". El Palacio 41/14-16: 71-74, 1936.
Believed to be caused by the breath of taboo animals and to be kindred disorders. Description of "turning the basket" ceremony and, in case of recurrence, the "circle of arm" ritual.

747. KANE, HENRY: "The Apache Secret Devil Dance". El Palacio 42/16-18: 93-94, 1937.
Description of the Ghan Dance by a San Carlos Apache student. This dance is treatment for "diseases of the nerves and mind... the dance is a form of prayer" (p. 94).

748. KLAH, HOSTEEN: Navaho Creation Myth. Santa Fe: Museum of Navaho Ceremonial Art, 1942.
The myth as recounted by an outstanding Navajo singer and weaver.

749. KLUCKHOHN, CLYDE: "Navaho Women's Knowledge of Their Song Ceremonials". El Palacio 45/21-23: 87-92, 1938.
In the Ramah-Atarque area, women had less participation than men as particpants in the Navajo religious system, both in theory and practice, age group for age group.

750. MATTHEWS, WASHINGTON: Navajo Legends. Memoirs of the American Folklore Society, 5, 1897.

751. MOONEY, JAMES: "The Jicarilla Genesis". AA Old Series 11/7: 197-209, 1898.
Origin Myth of the Jicarilla Apaches.

752. MORGAN, WILLIAM: "Navajo Treatment of Sickness". AA 33/3: 390-402, 1931.
Relationship of dreams to diagnosis.

753. MORGAN, WILLIAM: "Navajo Dreams". AA 34/3: 390-405, 1932.
Symbolism of dreams and their relation to religion.

754. OPLER, MORRIS E.: "The Concept of Supernatural Power Among the Chiricahua and Mescalero Apaches". AA 37/1: 65-70, 1935.

755. OPLER, MORRIS E.: "Some Points of Comparison and Contrast Between the Treatment of Functional Disorders by Apache Shamans and Modern Psychiatric Practice". American Journal of Psychiatry 92: 1371-1387, 1936.

756. OPLER, MORRIS E.: <u>Myths and Tales of the Jicarilla Apache Indians</u>. Memoirs of the American Folklore Society 31/6, 1938.

757. OPLER, MORRIS E.: "A Mescalero Apache Account of the Origin of the Peyote Ceremony". <u>El Palacio 52/19: 210-212, 1945</u>.

758. OPLER, MORRIS E.: "Reaction to Death Among the Mescalero Apache". <u>SWJA 2/4: 454-467, 1946</u>.
Morris Opler was the main researcher for the Jicarilla, Mescalero and Chiricahua Apaches.

759. REICHARD, GLADYS A.: <u>Navajo Medicine Man</u>. New York: J.J. Augustin, 1939.

760. ROESSEL, ROBERT A. and DILLON PLATERO, eds.: <u>Coyote Stories of the Navaho People</u>. Rough Rock, Arizona: Navaho Curriculum Center., 1968.

761. SPENCER, KATHERINE: <u>Reflection of Social Life in the Navaho Origin Myth</u>. Albuquerque: UNM Publication in Anthropology, No. 3, 1947.
A remarkable study about the links between historic experience and myth.

762. WYMAN, LELAND C. and FLORA L. BAILEY: "Two Examples of Navaho Physiotherapy". <u>AA 46/3: 329-337, 1944</u>.
Treatment of symptoms by physical manipulation.

4. <u>HISPANO</u>

763. BATCHEN, LOU SAGE: <u>Las Placitas: Historical Facts and Legend</u>. Placitas: Tumbleweed Press, 1972.
Stories collected under the WPA Writers' Project of the 1930's were published under sponsorship of the Placitas Garden Club.

764. BORHEGYI, STEPHEN F. DE: "The Cult of Our Lord of Esquipulas in Middle America and New Mexico". <u>El Palacio 61/12: 387-401, 1954</u>.
Close parallels between a Guatemalan miraculous healing shrine and the Santuario de Chimayó suggest that Chimayó, unique as a healing shrine in New Mexico, had direct influence from Guatemala.

765. CAMPA, ARTHUR: <u>Treasure of the Sangre de Cristos</u>.
Norman: University of Oklahoma Press, 1963.
Tales and traditions of hidden treasure.

766. CHAVEZ, TIBO: "Early Witchcraft in New Mexico".
<u>El Palacio 76/3: 7-9, 1970</u>. A 1733 case in Isleta in which
an Indian was accused of bewitching settlers; relationship
between disease symptoms and witchcraft fears.

767. ESPINOSA, AURELIO M: <u>Cuentos Populares Españoles, 3 vols</u>.
Stanford: Stanford University Press, 1923-1926.

768. ESPINOSA, AURELIO M: "Spanish Folklore in New Mexico".
<u>NMHR 2/2: 135-155, 1926</u>.

769. FOSTER, GEORGE M.: "Relationships Between Spanish and
Spanish-American Folk Medicine". <u>Journal of American Folklore
66/3: 201-217, 1953</u>.
An indispensable work for study of folk medicine in New Mexico.

770. RAEL, JUAN B.: <u>Cuentos Españoles de Colorady y de Nuevo
Mejico</u>. Stanford: Standford University Press, 2 vols. 1957.
518 tales collected in Colorado and New Mexico in 1930 and
1940, many previously published in the Journal of American
Folklore. A continuation of Aurelio Espinosa's pioneering
work; see 767, 768.

VII-H. <u>PLANTS, ANIMALS AND FOOD</u>

1. <u>GENERAL</u>

771. NEW MEXICO DEPARTMENT OF VOCATIONAL EDUCATION: <u>Vegetable
Dyes Bulletin</u>. Santa Fe, 1934 (Revised 1935).
One of the unpublished studies available in many libraries in
New Mexico, with information for the textile artist.

772. SCHOENWETTER, JAMES: <u>Amateur Botany in New Mexico</u>.
Santa Fe: MNM Press, PSP 6, 1964.
Popular pamphlet.

2. PUEBLO

773. BELL, WILLIS H. and EDWARD F. CASTETTER: The Utilization of Mesquite and Screwbean by the Aborigines in the American Southwest. Albuquerque: UNM Biological Series, Bulletin No. 5/5, 1941.

774. CASTETTER, EDWARD F.: Uncultivated Native Plants Used as Sources of Food. Albuquerque: UNM Biological Series, Bulletin No. 4/1, 1935.
Alphabetical listing by scientific name and grouping according to use by Pueblo Indians. Data on preparation methods.

775. CASTETTER, EDWARD F. and WILLIS H. BELL: The Aboriginal Utilization of the Tall Cacti in the American Southwest. Albuquerque: UNM Biological Series, Bulletin No. 5/1, 1937.

776. CASTETTER, EDWARD F., WILLIS H. BELL and ALVIN R. GROVE: The Early Utilization and Distribution of Agave in the American Southwest. Albuquerque: UNM Biological Series, Bulletin No. 5/4, 1938.

777. COLTON, MARY-RUSSELL F.: Hopi Dyes. Flagstaff: Museum of Northern Arizona, Bulletin 41, 1965.

778. CUSHING, FRANK: Zuñi Breadstuff. New York: Museum of the American Indian, Indian Notes and Monographs, Vol. 8, 1920.
A great classic by an early participant observer.

779. DEHUFF, ELIZABETH WILLIS: "Fiesta Foods". New Mexico Magazine 17/2: 21, 34-36, 1939.
Recipes for bread, tortillas, paperbread, posole, pinole and other corn dishes.

780. HUGHES, PHYLLIS, editor and compiler: Pueblo Indian Cookbook. Santa Fe: MNM Press, 1972.
Savory recipes from the Pueblos, charming illustrations by the editor.

781. ROBBINS, WILFRED W., JOHN P. HARRINGTON and BARBARA FREIRE-MARRECO: Ethnobotany of the Tewa Indians. BAE Bulletin No. 55, 1916.
An encyclopedic work including Tewa terminology.

782. WHITING, ALFRED E.: *Ethnobotany of the Hopi*. Flagstaff: Museum of Northern Arizona, Bulletin No. 15, 1939.

3. NAVAJO-APACHE

783. BAILEY, FLORA L.: "Navaho Foods and Cooking Methods". *AA 42/2: 270-290, 1940*.
Traditional foods, especially those used at feasts during sings.

784. BRYAN, NONEBAH and STELLA YOUNG: *Navajo Native Dyes*. U.S. Office of Indian Affairs, Education Division, Indian Handicraft Pamphlets, 1940.

785. ELMORE, FRANCIS H.: *Ethnobotany of the Navajo*. Santa Fe: SAR Monograph No. 9, 1944.

786. ELMORE, FRANCIS H.: "Food Animals of the Navajo". *El Palacio 44/22-24: 149-154, 1958*.

787. VESTAL, PAUL A.: *Ethnobotany of the Ramah Navaho*. Cambridge: PPMAAE 40/4, 1952.
Includes material from field notes of Bailey, Kluckhohn, Tschopik and Wyman and covers the following uses of plants: food, medicine, dyes, ceremony, smoking, string and rope making, basketry, toilet accessories, household articles, fuel, arrow poison. Techniques of growing cultivated plants are included.

788. WYMAN, LELAND C. and S. K. HARRIS: *Navajo Indian Medical Ethnobotany*. Albuquerque: UNM Bulletin, Anthropological Series, 4/1, 1941.

789. YOUNG, STELLA: *Native Plants Used by the Navajo*. Washington, D.C.: Office of Indian Affairs, 1938.

790. YOUNG, STELLA: *Navajo Native Dyes*. Washington, D.C.: Office of Indian Affairs, Native Handicrafts, No. 2, 1940.

4. HISPANO

791. BREWSTER, MELA SEDILLO: *A Practical Study of the Use of Natural Vegetable Dyes in New Mexico.* Albuquerque: UNM Bulletin No. 306, 1937.

792. BOYD, E.: *Indigo.* Santa Fe: MNM Press, 1962.

793. C. DE BACA, MARGARITA: *New Mexico Dishes.* Santa Fe: Rydal Press, 1966.

794. CAMPA, ARTHUR L.: "Piñon as an Economic and Social Factor". *New Mexico Business Review* 1/4: 144-147, 1932.

795. CAMPA, ARTHUR L.: "Chile in New Mexico". *New Mexico Business Review* 3/2: 61-63, 1934.

796. CURTIN, LENORE S. M.: *Healing Herbs of the Rio Grande.* Santa Fe: Laboratory of Anthropology, 1947.
Deals mainly with Hispano plant medicine, some information on the Pueblos.

797. GILBERT, FABIOLA C. DE BACA: *Historic Cookery.* Santa Fe: Published by "The Shed" (reprint), 1965.

798. STEWART, ELOISA DELGADO DE: *El Plato Sabroso Recipes.* Santa Fe: Ortiz Printing Shop (13th edition), 1972.

VII-I. WARFARE AND HUNTING

1. GENERAL

799. HONEA, KENNETH: *Early Man Projectile Points in the Southwest.* Santa Fe: MNM Press, Popular Series, Pamphlet No. 4, 1965.

800. PECKHAM, STEWART: *Prehistoric Weapons in the Southwest.* Santa Fe: MNM Press, PSP No. 3, 1965.
Both of the above popular pamphlets, while focussed on prehistoric times, provide worthwhile data for the historic period.

2. PUEBLO

801. ELLIS, FLORENCE H.: "Patterns of Aggression and War Cult in Southwestern Pueblos". SWJA 7/2: 177-201, 1951.
Pueblo social channelling of aggression includes village-sanctioned forms of punishment for competitive behavior, as well as the specialized functions of the War Priest.

802. KAY, ELEANOR: "The War Priest's Magic". New Mexico Magazine 20/6: 21, 34, 1942.
Zuñi Pueblo prepares for the draft of its young men. Description of the use of fetishes for hunting and war.

3. NAVAJO-APACHE (See Hill 72, 73)

803. OPLER, MORRIS E.: "A Chiricahua Apache's Account of the Geronimo Campaign of 1886". NMHR 13/4: 360-386, 1938.

4. HISPANO

804. COLLEY, CHARLES C.: "La Jineta: The Art of Moorish Horsemanship in the New World". El Palacio 76/2: 31-35, 1969.

5. ANGLO (see Sections III-D and IV-B and -D)

VII-J. RECREATION: GAMES, RIDDLES, JOKES

1. PUEBLO

805. FOX, ROBIN: "Pueblo Baseball: A New Use for Old Witchcraft". Journal of American Folklore 74/291: 9-16, 1961.
Power of public opinion in relation to witchcraft fears in the Pueblos: words have power and "bad thoughts and drunkenness let loose aggressive impulses which are feared. Baseball provides a potentially therapeutic avenue for competition and aggression.

806. GOGGIN, JOHN M.: "A Ball Game at Santo Domingo". AA 42/2, Part 1: 364-366, 1940.
Interesting Corollary to 805.

807. HARRINGTON, JOHN P.: "The Tewa Indian Game of "Cañute" ". AA 14/2: 243-286, 1912.
A study in extensive detail.

808. HODGE, FREDERICK WEBB: "A Zuñi Foot-Race". AA Old Series 3/3: 227-231, 1890.

809. KEECH, ROY A.: "The Kick-Stick Race at Zuñi". El Palacio 37/7-8: 61-64, 1934.

2. NAVAJO-APACHE

810. ABERLE, DAVID F.: "Mythology of the Navaho Game Stick-Dice". Journal of American Folklore 55/217: 144-155, 1942.

811. MINDELEFF, COSMOS: "Navajo Indian Gamblers". Scientific American 27 (July 8), 1899.

3. HISPANO

812. COBOS, RUBEN: "The New Mexican Game of Valse Chiquiao". California Folklore Quarterly, 1956.

813. NEW MEXICO WRITERS' PROJECT: The Spanish-American Song and Game Book. Albuquerque: UNM Press, 1942.
Traditionally, recreation and learning were combined in large family groups, as reflected in the description of games. Presently out of print, this work will soon be republished.

VIII. APPOINTED AND ELECTED GOVERNORS OF NEW MEXICO (1598-1974)

Under Spanish Rule

1598-1608	Don Juan de Oñate
1608-1610	Don Cristóbal de Oñate
1610-1614	Don Pedro de Peralta
1614-1618	Almirante don Bernadino de Zaballo
1618-1625	Don Juan de Eulate
1625-1629	Almirante don Felipe Sotelo-Ossorio
1629-1632	Capt. don Francisco Manuel de Silva Nieto
1632-1635	Capt. don Francisco de la Mora y Zaballos
1635-1637	Capt. don Francisco Martinez de Baeza
1637-1641	Capt. don Luis de Rosas
1641-	General don Juan Flores de Sierra y Valdéz
1641-1642	1st Sargento Francisco Gómez (or the Cabildo de Santa Fe)
1642-1644	Capt. don Alonzo Pacheco de Heredia
1644-1647	Capt. don Fernando de Argüello Caravajal
1647-1649	Capt. don Luís de Guzmán y Figueroa
1649-1653	Capt. don Hernando de Ugarte y la Concha
1653-1656	Don Juan de Samaniego y Xaca
1656-1659	Capt. don Juan Manso de Contreras
1659-1661	Capt. don Bernardo López de Mendizábal
1661-1664	Capt. don Diego Dionisio de Peñalosa Briceño y Berdugo
1664-1665	Capt. don Juan Miranda
1665-1668	Capt. don Fernando de Villanueva
1668-1671	Capt. don Juan de Medrano y Mesía
1671-1675	General don Juan Durán de Miranda (2nd time)
1675-1677	Capt. Don Juan Francisco de Treviño
1677-1683	Capt. don Antonio de Otermín
1683-1686	Capt. don Domingo Jironza Pétriz de Cruzate
1686-1689	Don Pedro Reneros de Posada
1689-1691	Capt. don Domingo Jironza Pétriz de Cruzate
1691-1697	Don Diego de Vargas Zapata Lujan de Ponce de León
1697-1703	Don Pedro Rodriguez Cubero
1703-1704	Don Diego de Vargas Zapata Lujan de Ponce de León, Marqués de la Nava Brazinas (2nd time)
1704-1705	Capt. don Juan Páez Hurtado
1705-1707	Don Francisco Cuervo y Valdéz
1707-1712	Almirante don José Chacon Medina Salazar y Villasen, Marqués de las Peñuelas
1712-1715	Don Juan Ignacio Flores Mogollón
1715-	Capt. don Felipe Martínez
1717-	Capt. don Juan Páez Hurtado (acting)
1717-1722	Capt. don Antonio Valverde y Cossio
1722-1731	Don Juan Domingo de Bustamante
1731-1736	Don Gervasio Cruzat y Góngora
1736-1739	Don Henrique de Olavide y Michelena
1739-1743	Don Gaspar Domingo de Mendoza
1743-1749	Don Joaquin Codallos y Rabál
1749-1754	Don Tomás Veles Cachupin
1754-1760	Don Francisco Antonio Marin de Valle

1760-	Don Mateo Antonio de Mendoza
1760-1762	Don Manuel de Portillo y Urrisola
1762-1767	Don Tomás Veles Cachupin (2nd time)
1767-1778	Capt. don Pedro Fermin de Mendinueta
1778-	Don Francisco Trebol Navarro
1778-1788	Teniente Col. don Juan Bautista de Anza
1788-1794	Don Fernando de la Concha
1794-1805	Teniente Col. don Fernando Chacón
1805-1808	Col. don Joaquin del Real Alencaster
1808-	Don Alberto Maynéz
1808-1814	Teniente Col. don José Manrique
1815-1816	Don Alberto Maynéz (2nd time)
1816-1818	Don Pedro Maria de Allande
1818-1822	Capt. don Facundo Melgares

Under Mexican Rule

1822-	Francisco Xavier Chávez
1822-1823	Col. José Antonio Vizcarra
1823-1825	Bartolomé Baca
1825-	Col. Antonio Narbona
1827-1829	Manuel Armijo
1829-1832	José Antonio Chávez
1832-1833	Santiago Abreu
1833-1835	Francisco Sarracino
1835-1837	Col. Albino Pérez
1837-1844	Manuel Armijo (2nd time)
1844-	Mariano Chávez (acting)
1844-	Felipe Sena (acting)
1844-1845	General Mariano Martinez de Lejanza
1845-	José Chávez y Castillo
1845-1846	Manuel Armijo (3rd time)
1846-	Juan Bautista Vigil y Alarid (acting)

Under United State Rule--Military

1846-	Gen. Stephen W. Kearny
1846-1848	Col. Sterling Price

Civil

1846-1847	Charles Bent
1847-1848	Donaciano Vigil

Civil Military Rule

1848-1849	Col. J. M. Washington
1849-1851	Col. John Munroe

Territorial Governors

1851-1852	James S. Calhoun
1852-	John Greiner (acting)
1852-1853	William Carr Lane
1853-	W. S. Messervy (acting)
1853-1856	David Merriwether
1856-1857	W. W. H. Davis (acting)
1857-1861	Abraham Rencher
1861-1866	Henry Connelly
1866-	W. F. M. Arny (acting)
1866-1869	Robert Mitchell
1869-1871	William A. Pile
1871-1875	Marsh Giddings
1875-	William G. Ritch (acting)
1875-1878	Samuel B. Axtell
1878-1881	Lew Wallace
1881-1885	Lionel A. Sheldon
1885-1889	Edmund G. Ross
1889-1893	L. Bradford Prince
1893-1897	William T. Thornton
1897-1906	Miguel A. Otero
1906-1907	Herbert J. Hagerman
1907-	J. Wallace Reynolds (acting)
1907-1910	George Curry
1910-1912	William J. Mills

State Governors

1912-1917	William C. McDonald
1917-	Ezequiel Cabeza de Baca
1917-1919	Washington E. Lindsay
1919-1921	Octaviano A. Larrazolo
1921-1923	Merrit C. Mechem
1923-1925	James F. Hinkle
1925-1927	Arthur T. Hannett
1927-1931	Richard C. Dillon
1931-1933	Arthur Seligman
1933-1935	A. W. Hockenhull
1935-1938	Clyde Tingley
1939-1942	John E. Miles
1943-1946	John J. Dempsey
1947-1950	Thomas J. Mabry
1951-1954	Edwin L. Mechem
1955-1956	John Simms
1957-1958	Edwin L. Mechem
1959-1960	John Burroughs
1961-1962	Edwin L. Mechem (appointed U.S. Sen. in Nov.)
1962-	Tom Bolack (Dec.)
1963-1966	Jack M. Campbell
1967-1970	David Cargo
1971-1974	Bruce King

IX. MUSEUMS IN NEW MEXICO

Following is a listing of museums in New Mexico for which information is available. Location is given, followed by the administrative authority in parentheses, and the type of museum facility.

ABIQUIU
    Ghost Ranch Museum (National Forest Service) Natural History, Zoo

ALAMOGORDO
    White Sands National Monument (N.P.S) Natural History

ALBUQUERQUE
    Museum of Albuquerque (Municipal) General
    Sandia Atomic Museum (U.S. Army) Science
    Sandia Park Museum (Private) History
    Telephone Museum (Mountain Bell) Telephonic History
    University of New Mexico:
        University Art Museum
        Southwest Biology Museum
        Geology Museum
        Jonson Art Gallery
        Maxwell Museum of Anthropology

ARTESIA
    Artesia Historical Museum and Art Center (Municipal) General

AZTEC
    Aztec Ruins National Monument (N.P.S.) Archaeological

BERNALILLO
    Coronado State Monument (Mus. of N.M.) Archaeological

CAPULIN
    Capulin Mountain National Monument (N.P.S.) History, Natural History

CARLSBAD
    Carlsbad Caverns National Park (N.P.S.) Geology, Natural History
    Carlsbad Library-Museum (Municipal) General

CHACO CANYON
    Chaco Canyon National Monument (N.P.S.) Archaeological

CHICO
    Dorsey Mansion, Historic House Museum (Private) History

CIMARRON
    Old Mill Museum (Private) History
    Ernest Thompson Seton Memorial Library and Museum
        (Boy Scouts of America) History, Ethnology

DEMING
    Chamber of Commerce Museum (Municipal) Natural History

DULCE
    Jicarilla Apache Tribal Museum (Jicarilla Council)
        History, Ethnology

FORT SUMNER
    Fort Sumner State Monument (Mus. of N.M.) History

GALLUP
    Gallup Museum (Chamber of Commerce) History, Anthropology

GILA HOT SPRINGS
    Gila Cliff Dwelling National Monument (N.P.S) Archaeology,
        Natural History

GRANTS
    Chamber of Commerce Geology Museum (Chamber of Commerce)
        Geology, Anthropology

JEMEZ SPRINGS
    Jemez State Monument (Mus. of N.M.) History, Archaeology

LAS CRUCES
    N.M. State University Museum General

LAS VEGAS
    Rough Riders Memorial and City Museum *Municipal) History

LINCOLN
    Lincoln County Courthouse Museum (State) History

LOS ALAMOS
    Los Alamos County Museum (Municipal) History, Anthropology
    Los Alamos Science Hall and Museum (Los Alamos Scientific
        Lab., U. of Calif.) Science

MADRID
    Old Coal Mine Museum (Private) History

MESILLA
    Gadsden Museum (Private) History

MORIARTY
    Longhorn Ranch and Museum of the Old West (Private) History

MOUNTAINAIR
    Abo State Monument (Mus. of N.M.) History, Archaeology
    Gran Quivira National Monument (N.P.S) as above
    Mountainair Museum (Private) History
    Quarai State Monument (Mus. of N.M.) History, Archaeology

PECOS
    Pecos National Monument (N.P.S.) History, Archaeology

PENASCO
    Picuris Pueblo Museum (Picuris Pueblo Council) History,
        Ethnology

PORTALES
    Anthropology Museum (E.N.M.U.) Anthropology
    Blackwater Draw Museum (E.N.M.U.) Archaeology
    Miles Museum of Minerology (E.N.M.U.) Geology

RAMAH
    El Morro National Monument (N.P.S.) History, Natural History

RATON
    Raton Museum (Historical Society) History

ROSWELL
    Roswell Museum and Art Center (Municipal) General

SANTA FE
- Bandelier National Monument (N.P.S.) Archaeology
- Chapel of San Miguel (Church) History
- Institute of American Indian Arts (Bureau of Indian Affairs) Art
- International Institute of Iberian Colonial Art (College of Santa Fe) Art history
- La Cienega, Spanish Colonial Outdoor Museum (Private) History
- Military Museum (National Guard) History
- Museum of Navaho Ceremonial Art (Foundation) Archaeology, Ethnology
- Museum of New Mexico
    - Anthropology Lab.
    - Fine Arts Museum
    - Museum of International Folk Art
    - Palace of Governors, History, Ethnology

AUTHOR INDEX

ABERLE, David F.: 443, 810
ABERT, Lt. J.W.: 303
ADAIR, John: 403, 460, 589
ADAMS, Eleanor B.: 224, 257, 258, 259, 260, 651
AGOGINO, George A.: 110
AHLBORN, Richard E.: 652
ALLEN, John E.: 102
ALLER, Paul and Doris: 662
AMBLER, J. Richard: 188
AMSDEN, Charles A.: 124, 545
ANDERSON, Frank G.: 419
ANONYMOUS: 680, 681
APPLEGATE, Frank: 420, 723
ARNOLD, Eliot: 304, 333
ARROWSMITH, Rex: 90
ASTROV, Margot: 671, 737
ATENCIO, Thomas C.: 347

BACA: Edwin: 498
BAHTI, Tom: 523, 672
BAILEY, Flora L.: 67, 738, 762, 783
BAILEY, L.R.: 249
BALDWIN, Brewster: 100
BANCROFT, Hubert H.: 29
BANDELIER, Adolph A.: 30, 31, 32, 41, 125
BANNISTER, B.: 27
BARKER, Ruth Laughlin: 553
BARTER, E.R.: 194
BASEHART, Harry W.: 454
BATCHEN, Lou Sage: 763
BELL, Willis H.: 773, 775, 776
BENAVIDES, Fray Alonso de: 261, 262
BENEDICT, Ruth: 724
BENNETT, Edna Mae: 590
BENNETT, Kay: 444
BERNSTEIN, Harry: 495
BINNER, Witter: 329
BIRRELL, Verla: 560
BLACK, Mary: 561
BLACKMAR, Frank W.: 348
BLAWIS, Patricia Bell: 461
BLOOM, John P.: 305

BLOOM, Lansing B.: 5, 263, 554
BLUHM, E.: 192, 193
BOLTON, Herbert E.: 1, 214, 264
BORHEGYI, Stephen F. de: 653, 764
BOURKE, John G.: 334, 739
BOWDEN, J.J.: 265
BOYD, E: 524, 555, 561, 618, 619, 620, 621, 622, 623, 654, 792
BOYD, Nathan E.: 395
BRACK, Gene: 496
BRADFIELD, Wesley: 184
BRAND, Donald D.: 126, 497
BRAYER, Herbert O.: 330, 349
BREITENBACH, E.: 633
BREWSTER, Mela Sedillo
    see Sedillo, Mela
BRODY, J.J.: 134
BROWN, Marie Hamilton: 725, 726
BRUGGE, David M.: 6, 250
BRYAN, Kirk: 111
BRYAN, Nonebah: 784
BULLARD, W.R.: 127
BUNKER, Robert: 404
BUNTING, Bainbridge: 91, 641, 655
BUNZEL, Ruth L.: 567, 682
BURGH, Robert F.: 158

C. DE BACA, Margarita: 793
CAHN, Edgar S.: 405
CAMPA, Arthur L.: 2, 706, 707, 708, 709, 710, 765, 794, 795
CAMPBELL, John M.: 112
CAREY, Frances: 33
CARLSON, Vada: 445
CARR, Malcolm: 68
CARROLL, H. Bailey: 266
CARSON, Christopher: 306
CASSIDY, Ina Sizer: 525, 721
CASTAÑEDA, Pedro de: 215
CASTETTER, Edward F.: 773, 774, 775, 776
CATA, Regina Albarado de: 727
CERAM, C.W.: 22
CHALAPI: 692
CHANDLER, Alfred N.: 350

CHAPMAN, Charles E.: 3
CHAPMAN, Kenneth M.: 568, 569, 570, 571, 605, 644
CHAVEZ, Amada: 251
CHAVEZ, Fray Angelico: 4, 225, 260, 267, 268, 269, 270, 271, 272, 273
CHAVEZ, Tibo: 274, 766
CHRISTIANSEN, Paige W.: 107
CLARK, Ann Nolan: 33
CLARK, Robert E.: 331
CLARKE, Thelma: 727
CLEAVELAND, Agnes Morley: 378
CLENDENEN, N.W.: 179
COBOS, Ruben: 720, 812
COKE, Van Deren: 624, 634
COLLEY, Charles C.: 804
COLLIER, John: 42, 332, 406
COLTON, Harold S.: 606
COLTON, Mary-Russell F.: 777
CONCHA, Joseph L.: 673
CONRON, John P.: 641
COOK, Harold J.: 113
COOLIDGE, Dane: 379
CORBETT, John M.: 649
CORDOVA, Andrew: 36
CORRELL, J. Lee: 6
COSGROVE, C.B. and H.S.: 185
CREMONY, John C.: 336
CROSNO, Maude D. and Masters: 92
CURTIN, Lenore S.M.: 796
CUSHING, Frank: 778
CUTLER, H.: 192, 193

DAVISON, Marguerite P.: 562
DEHUFF, Elizabeth Willis: 683, 684, 728, 729, 779
DeVOTO, Bernard: 307
DIAZ, Albert J.: 7
DICK, Everett: 308
DICK, Herbert: 114, 209
DICKEY, Roland F.: 526
DITTERT, Alfred, Jr.: 169
DOCKSTADER, Frederick: 674
DONNELLY, Thomas C.: 35
DORSEY, George A.: 43
DOUGLAS, Frederick H.: 534, 539, 540, 541, 572
DOUGLAS, Harriet G.: 563
DOZIER, Edward P.: 44, 45, 226, 421

DOZIER, Thomas: 685
DUMAREST, Fa. Noel: 46
DUNHAM, Harold H.: 351
DUNN, Dorothy: 585
DUTTON, Bertha P.: 47, 143, 540, 601, 680
DYK, Walter: 69

EDDY, Frank W.: 48, 128, 129, 168
EGGAN, Fred: 49
EDMONSON, Monro: 462
ELLIS, Bruce: 212, 656
ELLIS, Florence Hawley: 112, 126, 130, 131, 132, 133, 134, 140, 229, 408, 422, 423, 429, 430, 498, 608, 744, 801
ELMORE, Francis H.: 785, 786
EMERY, Irene: 557, 564
ESPINOSA, Aurelio M.: 711, 767, 768
ESPINOSA, Gilberto: 274, 625
ESPINOSA, J. Manuel: 227, 275
ESPINOSA, Jose E.: 626

FARMER, Malcolm: 201, 642
FENTON, William N.: 424
FERDON, Edward N., Jr.: 135, 198
FERGUSSON, Erna: 34, 407, 675
FEWKES, J. Walter: 425
FISHER, Reginald G.: 657
FOLMER, Henri: 276
FORBES, Jack D.: 499
FOSTER, George M.: 769
FOSTER, James M., Jr.: 363
FOSTER, Roy W.: 103
FOX, Robin: 426, 730, 805
FRANCIS, E.K.: 500
FRAZER, Robert W.: 336
FREIRE-MARRECO, Barbara: 781
FRENCH, David H.: 427
FRENCH, William: 380
FULTON, Maurice G.: 369

GALENAL, Welton C.: 25
GALVEZ, Bernardo de: 277
GAMIO, Manuel: 501
GARCIA, Antonio: 688
GARDNER, Hamilton: 337
GARRARD, Louis: 309
GIBSON, Charles: 216

GIBSON, George R.: 310
GILBERT, Fabiola C. de Baca: 352, 797
GILLMOR, Frances: 502
GLADWIN, H.S.: 136
GODDARD, Pliny E.: 50
GOETZMAN, William H.: 311
GOGGIN, John M.: 806
GOLDFRANK, Esther: 51
GONZALEZ, Nancie L.: 463
GOODRICH, James W.: 353
GOODWIN, Grenville: 70, 693
GRANGE, R., Jr.: 192
GREEN, R.C.: 137
GREENLEAF, Richard: 278
GREEVER, William S.: 381
GREGG, Josiah: 312
GRISHAM, Glen: 475
GRISWOLD, Lester: 527
GROVE, Alvin R.: 776
GRUBBS, Frank H.: 382
GUNNERSON, Dolores A.: 202, 203, 238
GUNNERSON, James H.: 204, 238, 503
GUTHE, Carl E.: 573

HACKETT, Charles W.: 228, 279
HAFEN, Ann and LeRoy: 313
HAGGARD, J. Villasana: 266
HAILE, Father Berard: 740, 741, 742, 743
HAINES, Francis: 504, 505
HALL, Edward T., Jr.: 138, 205
HALL, Martin H.: 364
HALSETH, Odd S.: 428
HAMMACK, Laurens C.: 139, 608
HAMMOND, Blodwen: 455
HAMMOND, George P.: 35, 217, 280, 281, 282
HARLOW, Francis H.: 574, 575
HARPER, Allan G.: 36
HARRINGTON, John P.: 93, 781, 807
HARRIS, S.K.: 788
HAURY, Emil W.: 186
HAUSKINS, Eunice: 713
Hawley, Florence, see Ellis, Florence H.
HAYES, Alden: 211
HENDERSON, Alice Corbin: 464
HESSELDEN, Louis G.: 643

HESTER, James: 110, 236, 237
HEWETT, Edgar L.: 41, 141, 142, 143, 218, 657
HEYMAN, Max L.: 506
HIBBEN, Frank C.: 115, 116, 117, 126, 144, 145
HILL, Gertrude F.: 609, 613, 614
HILL, W.W.: 71, 72, 73, 74, 78, 446, 447, 507, 745, 746
HINTON, Harwood P., Jr.: 370
HODGE, Frederick W.: 508, 592, 593, 808
HOEBEL, E. Adamson: 256
HOLMES, Kenneth L.: 314
HONEA, Kenneth: 799
HORGAN, Paul: 37, 230, 231
HORN and WALLACE: 365, 366
HORN, Calvin: 396
HOUGLAND, Willard: 627
HUBBELL, Elbert: 663
HUGHES, Phyllis: 780
HUNT, Aurora: 397
HUNT, W. Ben: 594
HURT, Wesley R., Jr.: 431, 432

JACKSON, Donald: 315
JAMES, Rebecca: 558
JARAMILLO, Cleofes M.: 465, 466
JEANCON, Jean A.: 146, 147
JELINEK, A.J.: 187
JENNINGS, Jesse D.: 23, 118
JONES, Fayette: 94
JONES, Hester: 658
JONES, Oakah L.: 219
JOSEPHY, Alvin M., Jr.: 38
JUDD, Neil M.: 148, 645

KANE, Henry: 747
KAPPLER, Charles J.: 509
KAUT, Charles: 75
KAY, Eleanor: 802
KEECH, Roy A.: 809
KELEHER, William A.: 338, 354, 371, 383
KELLY, Henry W.: 283
KELLY, Lawrence: 339, 510
KENDALL, George W.: 316
KENNER, Charles L.: 252, 511
KENNY, John B.: 587, 588
KENT, Kate Peck: 535, 547
KEUR, Dorothy: 206, 207

KIDDER, Alfred V.: 149, 150, 239, 576
KILHAM, Frances: 565
KIMBALL, Solon T.: 448
KIRK, Ruth Falkenburg: 595
KLAH, Hosteen: 748
KLUCKHOHN, Clyde: 76, 77, 78, 79, 151, 409, 449, 694, 695, 705, 749
KLUCKHOHN, Florence R.: 467
KLUCKHOHN, Lucy W.: 78
KNOWLTON, Clark S.: 468
KOTTLOWSKI, Frank: 100, 102, 107
KRIEGER, Alex D.: 119
KUBLER, George C.: 659
KURATH, Gertrude P.: 232, 687, 688

La FARGE, Oliver: 512
LAMAR, Howard R.: 340, 398
LAMBERT, Marjorie F. (Tichy): 152, 173, 188, 565, 577
LANGE, Charles H.: 433, 434, 435, 689, 690
LARSON, Robert W.: 399
LECKIE, William H.: 367
LEHMER, Donald J.: 189
LEIGHTON, Alexander H.: 79
LEIGHTON, Dorothea: 77, 79
LEMOS, Pedro J.: 528
LEONARD, Olen: 469, 470
LEOPARD, Donald D.: 400
LEVY, Jerold E.: 80
LEWIS, Marvin: 95
LINDGREN, Raymond E.: 342
LISTER, Florence C.: 24, 584
LISTER, Robert H.: 24, 209, 584
LOOMIS, Charles P.: 470, 471, 472, 473, 474, 475
LOOMIS, Noel M.: 285, 317
LOONEY, Ralph: 39
LOYOLA, Sister Mary: 318
LUCERO-WHITE, Aurora: 712, 713
LUHAN, Mabel Dodge: 635

MAES, Ernest: 410, 476
MAGOFFIN, Susan Shelby: 319
MAJOR, Mabel: 8

MALONEY, Thomas J.: 477
MALOUF, Carling and A. Arline: 253
MANGELSDORF, Paul C.: 25
MAREAU, Helene: 713
MARINO, C.C.: 240
MARMON, Miriam A.: 686
MARRIOTT, Alice: 578
MARTIN, Paul S.: 190, 191, 192 193, 194
MASON, Otis T.: 536
MATHEWS, Tom W.: 178
MATHEWS, Truman: 660, 664, 665
MATSON, Daniel S.: 83, 221
MATTHEWS, Washington: 615, 696, 697, 750
MAUZY, Wayne: 646, 647
McALLISTER, David P.: 676
McCARTY, Frankie: 355
McCLUNEY, Eugene: 195
McCOY, Joseph G.: 384
McGARR, Cuvier: 666
McKENNA, James A: 96
McKIBBIN, Davidson B.: 513
McNEISH, Richard S.: 25
McNITT, Frank: 385, 548
McNUTT, C.H.: 153
MEADERS, Margaret: 411
MEIGS, John: 636
MERA, Harry P.: 154, 196, 537, 542, 549, 552, 579, 580, 596
MERK, Frederick: 320
MILLER, Mamie T.: 284
MILLS, George: 628
MINDELEFF, Cosmos: 650, 811
MINDELEFF, Victor: 648
MINGE, Ward Alan: 286
MITCHELL, Emerson Blackhorse: 450
MOHR, A.: 120
MONTGOMERY, Arthur: 105
MOONEY, James: 751
MOORHEAD, Max: 241, 287, 288, 514
MORGAN, William: 81, 752, 753
MORLEY, Syvanus G.: 667
MORRIS, Earl H.: 155, 156, 157, 158
MR. MOUSTACHE: 451
MUEHLBERGER, William: 106
MUNCH, Francis J.: 412
MURPHY, Lawrence R.: 515

NASATER, Abraham P.: 285
NEAL, Arminta: 582
NELSON, Nels C.: 159
MEUBAUER, L.W.: 668
NEW MEXICO ARTISTS: 637
NEW MEXICO ASSOCIATION ON
    INDIAN AFFAIRS: 529
NEW MEXICO DEPARTMENT OF
    VOCATIONAL EDUCATION
    BULLETINS, 530, 771
NEW MEXICO STATE LIBRARY: 9
NEW MEXICO STATE UNIVERSITY:
    559
NEW MEXICO WRITERS' PROJECT:
    813
NEWCOMB, Franc J.: 82, 698,
    699
NICHOLS, Dan: 700
NOEL, Theo: 368
NOLAN, Frederick W.: 372
NORBECK, Edward: 23
NORTHROP, S.A.: 97, 98

OBERG, Kalervo: 36, 478
O'BRYAN, Deric: 436
OLD MEXICAN: 452
OPLER, Morris E.: 84, 85, 86,
    516, 701, 702, 754, 755,
    756, 757, 758, 803
ORTEGA, Peter Ribera: 714, 715
ORTIZ, Alfonso: 52, 53
OSBORNE, Douglas: 160
OTERO, Miguel A.: 356

PARISH, William J.: 386,
    387, 388
PARKHILL, Forbes: 321
PARSONS, Elsie Clews:
    54, 55, 56, 57, 58, 437,
    610, 691
PEARCE, Thomas M.: 8, 99, 720
PEARSON, Jim B.: 358
PECKHAM, Stewart: 161, 197,
    198, 800
PERRIGO, Lynn I.: 289
PESO, Charles di: 199
PLATERO, Dillon: 760
PLOWDEN, William W., Jr.: 585
POLDEVAART, Arie W.: 401
PORTER, Clyde and Mae Reed:
    322

POTTER, Chester W.: 373
POWELL, Laurence C.: 10
PROVINSE, John H.: 448
PUCKETT, Fidelia M.: 290

RAEL, Juan B.: 18, 716, 717, 770
RASCH, Philip: 374, 375, 376, 377
REED, Erik K.: 87, 162, 163, 164,
    165, 182, 517
REEVE, Frank D.: 5, 40, 242, 243,
    244, 518, 519
REICHARD, Gladys: 88, 551, 703,
    759
REITER, Paul: 151, 177
RENDON, Gabino: 479
RENO, Philip: 323
REY, Agapito: 217, 281, 282
RICKEY, Don, Jr.: 342
RILEY, Carroll L.: 208
RINALDO, J.B.: 191, 192, 193, 194
RITTENHOUSE, Jack D.: 11, 12
ROAT, Evelyn: 612
ROBB, John D.: 389, 718
ROBBINS, Wilfred W.: 781
ROBERTS, Frank H.H., Jr.: 166
ROE, Frank G.: 520
ROEDIGER, Virginia: 543
ROESSEL, Robert: 760
ROMERO, Cecil V.: 291
RUPPE, R.J.: 167
RUSSELL, Carl P.: 324

SACCONAGHI, Charles D.: 13
SAMORA, Julian: 480
SAMPLE, L.L.: 120
SANCHEZ, George I.: 481, 482
SASAKI, Tom: 453, 454
SAUNDERS, Lyle A.: 14
SCHAAFSMA, Polly: 597, 598,
    599, 600, 601
SCHAEFER, Jack: 390
SCHILLING, John H.: 101, 104
SCHOENWETTER, James: 26, 168,
    169, 772
SCHOLES, France V.: 15, 233,
    292, 293, 294
SCHROEDER, Albert H.: 83, 210,
    220, 221, 245, 254
SEDILLO, Mela: 719, 791
SEKAQUAPTEWA, Helen: 438
SELLERS, E.H.: 121

SENTER, Donovan: 408, 483
SHALKOP, Robert L.: 629, 630
SHELBY, C.C.: 228
SHEPARD, Anna O.: 576
SHEPARDSON, Mary: 455
SHINER, Joel: 237
SIDES, Dorothy Smith: 602
SIEGEL, Bernard J.: 439
SIMMONS, Marc: 222, 295, 296, 297, 521, 661
SIMONS, Suzanne L.: 440
SIMS, Agnes: 611
SLOAN, John: 638
SMILEY, T.L.: 27
SMITH, Anne M.: 413, 414, 415
SMITH, Ralph A.: 325
SMITH, W.: 170
SMYTHE, Donald: 522
SNOW, David H.: 586
SON OF FORMER MANY BEADS: 456
SONNICHSEN, C.L.: 343
SPENCER, Katherine: 68, 761
SPICER, Edward H.: 416, 417
SPIER, Leslie L.: 441, 544
STALLINGS, W.S., Jr.: 172
STARK, Richard B.: 720
STEINER, Stan: 457, 484, 490
STEPHENSON, R.L.: 174
STEVENSON, Philip: 485
STEWART, Eloisa Delgado de: 798
STEWART, F.J.: 391
STIRLING, Matthew W.: 731
STUBBS, Stanley: 27, 59, 171, 172, 212
SULLY, John M.: 108
SUTHERLAND, Patrick: 105
SWADESH, Frances Leon: 486, 487, 488, 489

TAFT, Robert: 639
TALAYESVA, Don: 60
TANNER, Clara Lee: 531, 603, 604
TAYLOR, Marguerite W.: 358
TAYLOR, Morris F.: 344, 359, 360
THESES and DISSERTATIONS, UNM: 16
THOMAS, Alfred B.: 223, 255, 298, 299
THOMASSON, Carol J.: 17
THORPE, Heather: 566

TICHY, Marjorie F. (see Lambert)
TILLEY, Martha: 538
TOULOUSE, Joseph H., Jr.: 111, 174, 213
TSCHOPIK, Harry, Jr.: 552, 583
TULLY, Marjorie F.: 18
TWITCHELL, Ralph E.: 19, 402
TYLER, Hamilton A.: 732

UNDERHILL, Ruth: 458, 532, 533, 677
U.S. DEPARTMENT OF COMMERCE: 669
U.S. GEOLOGICAL SURVEY: 109
UTLEY, Robert M.: 345

VALDEZ, Luis: 490
VAN DRESSER, Peter: 491, 492
VAN STONE, Mary R.: 678
VAN VALKENBURGH, Richard F.: 246
VELARDE, Pablita: 733
VESTAL, Paul A.: 787
VESTAL, Stanley: 326
VIERRA, Carlos: 670
VILLAGRA, Gaspar Perez de: 300
VIVIAN, R. Gordon: 175, 176, 177, 178
VIVIAN, R. Gwinn: 179
VOGEL, Virgil J.: 722
VOGT, Evon Z.: 61, 403, 459

WADDISON, Jerold G.: 493
WADLEIGH, A.B.: 392
WAGNER, Henry R.: 20
WALLACE, Ernest: 256
WALLACE, William S.: 393, 394
WALLRICH, William: 494
WALTER, Paul A.F.: 234, 361
WALTERS, Frank: 640
WARREN, Helene: 581
WARREN, Nina Otero: 679
WATERS, Frank: 734
WATSON, Editha L.: 6
WEBER, David J.: 328
WEIGLE, Marta: 301
WENDORF, Fred: 180, 181, 182, 198
WENHAM, Edward: 631, 632
WESTPHALL, Victor: 362
WETHERHILL, Louisa Wade: 502
WETHERINGTON, Ronald K.: 183
WHEAT, Joe Ben: 200

WHITE, Leslie: 62, 63, 64, 65, 66, 235, 735
WHITING, Alfred E.: 782
WHITMAN, William: 442
WILDER, M.A.: 633
WILLEY, Gordon R.: 28
WILSON, John P.: 346
WITHERSPOON, Gary: 445
WOODBURY, Richard B. and Natalie F.S.: 170
WOODS, Betty: 704
WOODWARD, Arthur: 616
WOOLLEY, Doriane: 68
WORCESTER, Donald E.: 247, 248
WORMINGTON, H.M.: 122, 123, 582
WORTH, Sol: 460
WRIGHT, Barton: 612
WYMAN, Leland C.: 617, 695, 705, 762, 788

YOUNG, John V.: 575
YOUNG, Otis E.: 328
YOUNG, Robert W.: 89
YOUNG, Stella: 784, 789, 790

ZARATE SALMERON, Father Ceronimo de: 302
ZERWEKH, Sister Edward Mary: 418
ZIMMERMAN LIBRARY: 21
ZUNI PEOPLE, The: 736

www.ingramcontent.com/pod-product-compliance
Lightning Source LLC
Chambersburg PA
CBHW050502110426
42742CB00018B/3338